Tales I Tell My Mother

Tales I Tell My Mother

A collection of feminist short stories

by

Zoë Fairbairns
Sara Maitland
Valerie Miner
Michele Roberts
Michelene Wandor

The Journeyman Press
London / West Nyack

First published 1978 by the Journeyman Press
97 Ferme Park Road, Crouch End, London N8 9SA
and 17 Old Mill Road, West Nyack, NY 10994

ISBN 0 904526 34 8

The Journeyman Press would like to acknowledge *Spare Rib* and
Fireweed in which the following stories have appeared:

Right Hand on the Day of Judgement copyright © 1976 by Valerie Miner
Acts of Violence copyright © 1976 by Zoë Fairbairns
Womb with a View (as *Dreamlines*) copyright © 1976 by Michele Roberts
Radio Times copyright © 1976 by Michelene Wandor
After the Ball was Over copyright © 1977 by Sara Maitland
You Only Have to Say copyright © 1977 by Zoë Fairbairns

Photoset by Red Lion Setters Ltd, London, and
printed in Great Britain by Biddles Ltd, Guildford

Contents

Introduction

You don't have to read this introduction.

But since you are reading the book, it may be that you would like to know a little about who wrote it, how and why, what is intended and what isn't. We would like to tell you.

On the other hand, it may be that if you want to read short stories, then short stories are what you want to read. And either they are worth reading on their own merit, or they aren't. And if they aren't, then no amount of explanation, self-criticism, chat (or excuses) from the authors, is going to make you like them (stories or authors) any better. It's a valid point of view — one with which at least one member of the group has a sneaking sympathy — and you are hereby dismissed to read the stories.

But you are still here? Good. We are: five women, writers, feminists and socialists. It is possible that our definitions of those terms may differ from yours (and that includes the first term, for there are many definitions of 'real women' under which none of us would qualify) but that is how we define ourselves. We are Sara, Zoë, Michele, Michelene and Valerie, in no particular order. We might make suitable material for one of those old eleven-plus verbal reasoning tests:

S, Z, V, M1 and M2 are five feminists.
Three of them are or have been married.
Two of them are mothers.
Two of them share their homes with one man.
(Each.)
Three of them live with one or more women.
(Including daughters.)

ANSWER THE FOLLOWING QUESTIONS:

Which of them lives with a curate?
Which of them lives in Penge?

or

S, Z, V, M1 and M2 disagree among themselves as to:
Whether it is nice to have children
Whether housewives should get money for the work they do
Whether abortion should be freely available at 28 weeks
Whether people should get married
Whether God and Jesus Christ exist, and
Whether it matters.
What can they find to agree on?

Well—

Each of them knows for a fact that:
Everyone else in the group is in league to put her down.
This is the finest and best group of women anyone had the privilege of being
    supported by.
She is the best writer in the group, if not the world.
(Or the worst.)
She is unfeminist, unsisterly, unworthy of the others.
Nobody understands what she is on about, which is her failure.
Nobody understands what she is on about, which is their loss.

It is a great responsibility to have to introduce this group, being a member of it. Feminist collectives have their own etiquette, breaches of which can be just as embarrassing (even though just as unintended) as using the wrong fork used to be, or sitting when you're meant to kneel in church. For instance, if I reel off our respective marital statuses or living arrangements, am I committing the old sin of defining women by their family relationships? If I tell you what we do for our livings, am I being elitist? If I tell you what we look like, am I treating us as sex objects? Yet how can I introduce us without reference to these things? I hope you can appreciate the way I have skirted the problem, but I hope you also have some sense of being introduced.

And now the stories. They are arranged in sections, very loose themes drawing together the stories in each section. We do think this is important, and it has been interesting for us to see three themes emerging, unbidden; for it would be less than honest to pretend that the themes or the sections predated the stories. In the first section, we look at some of the things that happen when feminism meets the rest of the world head on. In the second, we look at what it's actually like to have your life changed by being in the women's movement. In the third, we look at how being in the movement affects the way people look at everyone and everything. We know that few people read a book of short stories from cover to cover; but you might like to try it.

We met in each other's homes to produce this book, at intervals of between one and three weeks. Stories were circulated amongst us in the intervals, and were then fully.discussed. Changes were usually made in the light of the discussions, and no story has been included that does not have the unanimous agreement of the group that it should be included; nevertheless, we believe that collectivity has its limits, and each story is ultimately the work of its individual author, and is signed as such.

Collectivity is a word that is bandied about a lot in the women's movement. Sometimes 'collective' is just a trendy euphemism for the same old committee. Sometimes it's an excuse for not doing anything. At its best though — and it has been good for us — it really can mean a group of equals, united by a genuine determination to get on with the job, and disciplined (in the sense of feeling strong obligation to do what you said you would do) by the simple realisation that, busy though I am, and valuable as my other work may be, it is no more so than hers; and I have no right to waste her time by deeming my time to have priority. The word is respect. It's not a thing women are generally taught to have for each other. But it's basic if a collective is to function.

Early in the group's history, we had a lot of anguished discussion about how we could cope if a situation arose in which one member wrote, and liked, a story which everyone else thought was terrible. It was agreed in principle that the majority must prevail, but each of us secretly hoped it wouldn't arise. None of us wanted to be the spurned author. We wanted even less to be part of the collective signature on the rejection slip. But it has never come to this. Although a sixth potential member left the group after its first few meetings, this was her own choice, and was not connected with any 'rejection' of her work. For the rest of us, our criticisms have become more candid and less pussy-footing as we have gained confidence, but no-one has ever demanded a story's removal. What has happened — and it has happened at least once for each of us — is that we have offered to withdraw our stories when it has become clear that they didn't fit in.

Here, though, are the ones that (we think) did fit in. We hope you like them. And thank you for reading this.

Zoë Fairbairns

ONE

Feminist fiction and language

One sunny morning an elephant and a mouse go for a walk in the same jungle. They meet.
Elephant: You're very small.
Mouse: I've been ill.

Is there such a thing as 'feminist language'?

These short discussion pieces, which frame the three sections of the book, are individual commentaries on some of the most important issues we discussed while we were writing the stories. One question we kept returning to was whether our aim — to produce a collection of feminist fiction — entailed the development of a feminist language. Or indeed, whether there already was a feminist language which we could simply yoke to our purpose.

When the Women's Liberation Movement started (1969-70 in England), a lot of necessary rhetoric hit the stands:
Women have been silent, we said.
Women have been invisible, we said.
We will be heard, we will be seen, we asserted.

That rhetoric was part of the battering ram which began to break through the many barriers constraining women in our society; women began to speak to each other in a new way, to share and analyse experience, to develop a theory about women's position, and to act on and change that position in the whole of society. As the rhetoric was accompanied and followed by action, it came under question itself.

The idea that women have been 'silent', for example, means at least two things: firstly, a quite literal silence. Women have been largely absent (and therefore silent) from positions of power in all societies throughout history (of course when I say 'absent' I'm testing the rhetoric — because what I 'mean' is that women have not had equal status with men — in all social classes). Secondly, women's 'silence' is a more subtle thing; it is obviously true that girls and boys learn the same basic language, women talk, women write. But access to literacy has only recently become a potential for all members of society, with state education, and the fight for the equal right to education has been one fought for not only by the organised labour movement, but also by women of the middle classes.

The written and spoken language we learn is crucial to the way we perceive, 'name' and control the world we live in; access to education and knowledge are vital for groups who are oppressed in society, so that they can actively express and struggle for themselves. Because sexist ideology argues that women are 'naturally' inferior to men (across classes), even the day-to-day conversation of women is dismissed as trivial, gossip, women's talk — as implicitly inferior to the subjects that men choose to talk about.

And all this takes place in the same context: we all learn (more or less) the same basic English, grammar, sentence structure, all kinds of features which make it similar to the languages that people in other cultures use. In some ways English has an advantage in that it is less gender-bound than some other languages — French and German assign gender to inanimate objects, modern Hebrew gender-binds its verbs, according to the sex of the speaker and the person addressed. To what extent this gives English more potential for breakthroughs in challenging people to reassess their unthinking assumptions re men and women's roles, is an interesting question. Certainly if we accept the fact that the particular historic forms language takes both express and help form the ideas people have about the world, then a relatively gender-free language may be something to aim for.

Already feminists have challenged the more overt elements in the language which help perpetuate women's image as second-class citizens; the term 'mankind', meant to include the whole range of the human species ends up sounding as though women did not exist. Gender-neutral words are now being used when they can refer to members of either sex — 'people' instead of 'men', 'chairperson' instead of the more common 'chairman'. This 'feminese' also has a positive, innovative element: we have coined words like 'male chauvinism', 'sexism', which represent some of the complex concepts which feminists have developed in order to understand the mechanisms which maintain the idea that men are the superior sex. The story which opens the book, *Bus Ticket* illustrates the conflict which ensues when a woman refuses to be identified by her marital status ('Miss' or 'Mrs') and insists on the new 'Ms' which simply indicates that she is female. A simple change like that can act as a shock tactic on people who accept women's current secondary status as natural and inevitable.

The attacks on old words and the coining of new are the visible tip of the iceberg of change. More important in the longterm are the ways in which women make use of the existing language to reconstruct the submerged history of women throughout society, to show that women were indeed an active and vital half of the population, and to analyse the ways in which the sexual division of labour splits men and women into different social camps, and consistently says that the woman's world (whether out at work or at work in the home) is inferior to the man's world.

Alongside the reconstruction of history, is the use of the existing language to document and express the changes we are part of. We have chosen to use the language and form of the short story to evoke in this first section what happens when independent, feminist women come up against people and situations hostile to the 'new woman'.

Both *Womb with a View* and *The Right Hand on the Day of Judgement* are about women in different classes who are on the verge of asserting a new personal independence; in both cases feminism and the women's movement hover behind the main action, informing and influencing it. *Just Lie Back and Think of the Empire* is partly about a breakdown in communication when a feminist travels in another culture where women are treated quite crudely as sexual objects. Finally, *Acts of Violence* juxtaposes elements in an intertwined family drama which spins off from, and back to, the fierce contemporary arguments about abortion — a word whose meanings reverberate from 'murder' to 'liberation for women', depending on the political position its speaker holds.

I don't think there is any such thing as a 'feminist language' — or at any rate any language as such which can be clearly defined as feminist, as opposed to non-feminist. Even the newly coined words are made up of pre-existing elements — a language evolves and changes very slowly. Our challenge lies in the way we use the existing language to resurrect our submerged history, and convey our current feminist perspective on the world we live in. The surface meanings of the stories will be clear to anyone who can read English; whether they are successful in conveying a new perspective on fiction is up to you — the reader — to assess. These essays are intended to illuminate and provoke thought before and after you read the stories. Language is not always just what it says.

One sunny morning an elephant and a mouse go for a walk in the same
jungle. They meet.
Elephant: You're very small.
Mouse: I've been ill.

_____

Now rewrite this story in your own words.

                                                      Michelene Wandor

Bus Ticket
Zöe Fairbairns

This is a very short story about being in the women's movement every day
of your life.

I used to travel by bus a lot, so I had a season ticket. You had to sign
your name on the front, and you had to delete whichever does not apply
to you of 'Mr, Mrs or Miss'. None of them applied to me, so I deleted
them all and put 'Ms'.

Now 'Ms' was by then accepted — well, tolerated — by such prestig-
ious and indispensable bodies in Britain as the Inland Revenue, the
Guardian, the Passport Office, the Post Office, the Co-op Bank and
Hackney public library. I also had high hopes of the Electricity Board,
particularly as I had taken to cutting 'Miss' off my meter reading cards
with scissors and it was one of those cards you aren't allowed to cut or
mutilate as it upsets the computer. All this notwithstanding, 'Ms' was
not acceptable to the conductor of the No. 14 bus that Monday. He
snatched my ticket, demanded to know if I was Miss or Mrs, glanced at
my ringless left hand when I refused to answer, crossed out 'Ms' and
wrote 'Miss'.

I'm not what you'd call the retiring type, and I rarely flinch from a
fight when I'm sure of my own righteousness; but there is one thing I
cannot cope with, and that is unprovoked aggression. I am prepared to
accept that anyone who knows me may dislike me, but when someone
who *cannot* dislike me because they don't know me, attacks me, I
collapse inside, I lose eloquence, I get frightened, sometimes I cry. So I
said nothing to this conductor, just wrote down his staff number.

When it was time to get off the bus, he gave me what I thought was a
friendly smile, and said, 'It's all right, dear, I agree with you.' I was
encouraged. 'I don't know what you are,' he went on, 'I don't know if
you're a boy or a girl.' He then invited my fellow passengers to speculate
on the subject.

I left the bus, went to an inspector, reported the incident. He promised
to look into my complaint and ceremoniously restored my defaced

season ticket with a rubber. He suggested I confirm my complaint in writing.

I spent the day between anger and guilt. So what if I report him. So he gets disciplined or yelled at or fired. He's an oppressed worker doing a horrible job. Perhaps he heard today that he's going to be evicted, his mother's sick, his kid's been thrown out of school. Hasn't he got enough to worry about without being clobbered over the head by the injured pride of a woman fortunate enough to have the time and the brain to worry about the title on her season ticket?

Wouldn't the right thing be to write to London Transport withdrawing the complaint, and send a friendly letter to the conductor himself explaining the meaning of 'Ms' and asking his tolerance for opinions differing from his own?

Such thoughts soothed me, and then the reality of what had happened would come shooting through my consciousness like a speedboat churning up a calm sea: how *dare* he decree that I must wear a badge indicating, for men's convenience, whether I was available or already had an owner?

How dare he speculate on the subject, then write his conclusions on a document I must carry round with me and display for a month?

How dare he whip up strangers to hostility because I didn't wear clothes clearly indicating my sex — what was it to them whether I was a woman or a man?

Then I was showered with the realisation that I had spent half a working day thinking these thoughts, during which time, if I had put a foot wrong, I would have immediately proved, to some people's satisfaction, the innate unsuitability of women for this kind of work; and that clinched it; and I wrote the letter and confirmed the complaint. Wouldn't you?

There is now a space for 'Ms' on a London Transport bus season ticket.

The story is true. Every word. Well, not quite every word. You see, the conductor wasn't a he but a she. Which somehow makes it different and somehow doesn't. And I still don't know if what I did was right, or even worth the bother; and I still resent every minute I spend wondering.

Womb With a View
Michele Roberts

From the kitchen window you can see the whole of King's Cross station spread out underneath you: the massive iron and stone curve of the station building itself, the tatty warehouses and sheds. And then the railway lines themselves, snaking out secretly and backwards and then suddenly fanning out into a thousand arteries of shining black steel leaping through London and beyond to the places you can only imagine, the lines pulsing her brain with the excitement of where they're going.

Maggie's relation to them in space doesn't change that much; you can see them from the kitchen; you can't from the bedsitting room. When you're five flights down on the ground again you're only really conscious of the high brick wall opposite, and the noise. The railway lines define the neighbourhood all right: Railway Hotel on the corner that the Council's started using for temporary accommodation for other single mothers not so lucky as she, as the social worker kept telling her; Railway Cafe opposite the launderette with coloured transfers on the window and a goldfish tank next to the curry puffs and ketchup bottles. Railway Tavern where Ted sometimes drops in to meet her on Friday nights. The trains time her life, crashing through fitful dreams at night, slackening off in the early hours, roaring her out of bed in the mornings faster than any alarm clock. If she's in a good mood she'll time Ted's egg by the 8.05 to Edinburgh; on the other hand, on a bad day she'll shout at Ted to make his own bloody breakfast and curse at Frieda for wasting good food on her plate.

Maggie awoken from the damp heavy warmth of Ted's body dead in sleep and the blankets piled on the single bed with a dip in the middle brushes her hair and clutches back at the ribbon of dreams from the night before. Maggie awoken from dreams of flying, from dreams of women with long hair building houses of hair, sits on the lavatory calculating whether she can afford a new pair of tights this week. A crash on the stairs and a thumping on the door opposite jerks her attention back to the lavatory door which badly needs repainting. You're never alone in this world, away from other people's demands, except in the lavatory. And this one doesn't really count, considering it's shared with four other tenants. That'll be Jo, with her kid Lucy. Never late Jo is, half-past eight sharp like a bloody train steaming up and come on Maggie for Christ's sake they close the nursery doors at nine you should know that by now. OK, OK, I'm coming, put the milkbottles out, powder her nose, don't let the neighbours see you leave, Ted, can't trust them not to tell the welfare and get my money stopped, find Frieda's windcheater and out they go.

Out on the street the fog sears the back of your nostrils and the cold sticks a needle up every pore. You wouldn't know it was autumn except for the odd dry leaf blowing down the road from the cemetery. Kick in the gut from the air though, somehow. Twenty years ago she was Lucy and Frieda's age, putting on school uniform for the first day of the winter term, long serge skirt suddenly covering the scratched knees used to shorts, thick woolly stockings sliding strangely up the white smooth skin, nylon suspender belt holding in her stomach making her think of the opening under the dark bush below. Wonder if things will change for these two, twenty years on, poor little buggers. No fathers, and the nursery staff working devotedly to wipe out the evil influence of their feckless mothers. What with the wind and the trains and the traffic and her woollen hat pressed tightly over her ears it's hard to hear what Jo's saying. She yells back.

'What?'

'I said, are you coming to the meeting tonight?'

'What meeting?'

'The women's meeting, you dummy, that lot from the Charter, the Working Women's Charter or whatever they call it —'

'Oh, them —'

They'd met them in the pub a couple of weeks back. Long skirts, talking about unions and equal pay. Jo and Maggie and some of the others from work had gone back last week and met them again. They wanted to get them into a union, lots of ideas about what they could do for you. She hadn't really forgotten, hadn't wanted to think about it really. Anger of a kind; what could those girls, students most likely, know about her life, bloody cheek to come wading in and try and organise your life like that. They'd listened to what Jo had said though. Jo always had had the gift of the gab, she could make a stone laugh doing her imitation of Mr Silver trying to get her up behind the cloakroom door.

Maggie had stayed quiet, gone home thinking if you think you're oppressed mate then listen to this. And then back home with Ted and Frieda both asleep and Jo gone, it had all burst up in tears Maggie had

squashed down with cigarettes. What right did they have, that lot,
getting you to think about how bloody life was, sitting in this poky flat
with Ted always so tired he never played with Frieda or talked to herself
and fell asleep straight after having it off. And now here's Jo dancing
around saying come to another meeting.

'I don't know —' Maggie yells back as they cross the main road at a
run. 'Ted's got his union meeting tonight,' she lies, 'I'll have to be in
with Frieda. And anyway, there's a programme I wanted to watch —'

They're at the nursery. Quick kiss on the cheek for Lucy and Frieda,
watch their skinny legs scuttle across the yard and in through the
corrugated iron hut's battered doors. Quarter to nine. Time for a cup of
tea before they're due in down the road. Silvex Modes, do pop in, ladies,
convenient hours to suit you and the kiddies, and we'll lovingly screw you
over for fifty pence an hour. At least there's no awkward questions asked,
no needing to bother with insurance, does mean there's a bit to add to
her measly SS giro every week.

Jo and Maggie, both early twenties but looking thirty, dressed by jumble
sales as they can't afford Silvex Modes prices, gaze at each other over the
plastic pots of mustard on the formica table top.

'What's this programme then, lovey?'

'The Amazons, it's called. This woman says there's still some of them
around. You know, women with only one tit, they cut the other off so
they could shoot better with a bow and arrow, they live together, all
women and no men, this woman's written a play about them —'

Lovely face, Jo has, despite the lines and paleness, dark hair and blue
eyes, says she got them from her wild Irish grandmother. Not like her,
Maggie, she has to put a lot of effort into looking nice. Ted laughs at her,
putting on her warpaint he calls it, but he's pleased enough when all his
mates ogle her down the pub.

'Sounds pretty daft to me. Tell us about it if it's so important.'

Maggie sucks on a No.6.

'I don't know, just caught my imagination somehow, I suppose,
thought it might be a bit of a laugh. Reminded me of us, I suppose, girls
without men. And of those girls in the pub, it was one of them told me
about it —'

'So you have been thinking about them. Well, come on then, Maggie,
let's go then, shall we. They might be OK after all, hell, it's an evening
out at least —'

'I've told you, there's no-one to look after Frieda. All right for you
with Mrs Ash next door, you don't have to worry. Down the pub as often
as you want with all the fellers —'

'Bloody hell — I don't neglect that kid, I'm a good mother to her, I've a perfect right to go out of an evening. Stuck at work all day with no-one to come home to at night — all very well for you sitting holding hands with Ted with little Frieda watching, you don't know what it's like, being on your own, not really —'

Maggie's never told Jo how bad it's been recently with Ted. There are some things you just keep your mouth shut about and one of those is when sex isn't much good. Especially when you've always let on that it was great before.

'Don't I, hell — oh, go to hell —'

Jo's voice follows her heels clicking fast over the cafe's tiled floor.

'Maggie, you fucking idiot, come back, I'm sorry —'

Go anywhere, out of this whole mess. Except that she's got to clock in in five minutes time. All right for some on their autumn inter-city breaks. Get away from it all, he coos over the radio every morning, you ladies are so wonderful, you deserve a little luxury —

Silvex Modes is on the top floor of a decaying terrace house opposite the cafe. The council has it marked down for demolition, part of their plan for new accommodation for existing council tenants on either side. There's no hurry for that now that the money's been cut back, Mr Silver can go on economising on space and heat and lighting for his twelve women workers for a good few years yet, and in any case, no-one's been round to check up on him for a long time now.

Jo and Maggie are lucky, they've managed to swing it so that they work side by side. Hard to talk though; the machines are as noisy as the trains back at the flats and there's pop music screaming out all day long from the radio wedged on top of the mantelpiece. Dave Whatsit introducing all the records, voice like malted chocolate choking you with sweetness. You're so special ladies, just because you're you. As a mere male, what can I do but worship, you're all woman, every bit of you, the funny silly things you say and do.

Maggie's mum taught her how to sew, years ago, they had an old Singer from her aunt who died, and ran up the clothes for all the family. Maggie remembers one dress: it was plum velvet with lace all round the neck and cuffs, clutch bag to match. It took her a week to make, that dress, she'd made it specially for the dance at the police cadets' college, and then she'd been so shy she'd spent most of the evening in the Ladies. That was when she met Jo. Jo borrowed her lipstick and said she liked her dress, it had all started from there.

Their shift is from half-nine to half-two. Part-time work, so you can't expect the same rates as fulltimers would get. No point making a fuss; plenty more women with young kids anxious for work, as Mr Silver will explain to silence the muttering that occasionally drowns even the machines. Teabreak: Jo's fooling about as usual, pretending to be Princess Anne choosing a wedding dress from Silvex Modes. Queer how it gets us, all women and no men, the way we let off steam, like being back at school again, lifting up people's skirts in the cloakroom. Half-past two at last. Maggie's eyes and back are aching like hell. Good excuse to be grumpy and quiet while the others talk about the meeting and to avoid Jo's eyes, pretending not to hear her abrupt conversational openings. Maggie grabs her bag from the wire cage under her seat, throws on her coat and is down the stairs and out in the street before any of the others. First time in a year she hasn't waited for Jo so they can do their shopping together.

Maggie's gone the opposite way from Tesco's; her heels are sinking into grass. The park's empty at this time of day before the kids are let out of school. There's a big house at the end of an avenue of chestnuts. They store deckchairs in it now and in summer they have art exhibitions there. She hates parks; it takes half an hour to get there from the flats and then the kids are put inside one lot of railings like some kind of animals and you walk up and down inside another lot and watch them. The trees poise to eject leaves and hurl them at the wind, there is nobody in the big house to see the park's invasion by the people, the iron benches under the elms are empty, each foot curling into a clutch of leaves. Ladies, you're so wonderful, so smiling and serene. Except when I bleeding am then no-one knows anything's up, not even Jo. All this mud's going to ruin my shoes. Funny that Jo wanted me to come with her so much. Always thought I was the shy one of us two. But then she always thinks that I manage. Wind's colder now, you've got to be a kid to enjoy it, go shooting down the hill flailing your arms pretending to be an aeroplane. Maggie's sitting hunched up on the bench, its iron legs striking chilly through her tights, conker cases under her feet, cigarette between her lips. Wonder where Jo is.

Christ — look at the time — I'll be late collecting Frieda.

High heels stumbling over gravel, coat flying open. Three men, unemployed they must be, on the bench near the gate, smoking pitifully thin rollies, brighten up as she rushes past.

'Hey, love, what's the hurry? Lost your boy-friend, have you? Slow down, girl, he's not worth it —'

The nursery's doors and windows are shut, a sweet paper lurching in the wind the only movement in the yard. Then as her stomach jumps in panic, Maggie sees them in the far corner, Lucy and Frieda, with Jo beside them. Squatting to hug the two kids, fussing with Frieda's collar, unable to stop holding her in relief. Jo's voice comes down to her, gentle.

'It's OK, Maggie, I got here a bit late as well, but they were waiting, you didn't run away did you, loves? I was going to take them both back with me if you didn't turn up, I was going to get us fish and chips as a treat —'

Jo's talking even faster than usual, shows she's still feeling a bit down.

'Thanks, Jo.'

Maggie finishes tying Frieda's shoelace, stands up, meets Jo's eyes. They both know it'll be all right between them in a bit. Arm-in-arm back down the hill, kids hanging on one at each side. Funny that the kids are so quiet, usually after a day cooped up in there they're jumping around all over the place.

'Mum —'

It's Frieda, tugging at her hand.

'Yes, love?'

'Want some Smarties, like the man said —'

'What man, love?'

'The funny man, Uncle Funny —'

'What man? There aren't any men in the nursery — Frieda — what've you been doing? Who're you talking about?'

Maggie's shaking Frieda, who starts howling. Jo's clutching Maggie's arm.

'It's all right, Maggie, I was going to tell you when we got home, shut up will you, the kids are all right I tell you —'

Jo's organising them all, down the hill at a brisk pace, impossible to talk while you time a dash across the road scooping the kids up with you as lorries thunder in both directions farting diesel fumes into your face. Out into the street again from the chippie, warm smelly parcel telling your hands and nose you're still alive, feet remembering as they do every day to avoid the broken-up pavement in front of the pub. Steam on the kitchen window cuts off the railway lines, making the tiny kitchen for once a friendly place. Jo and Maggie sitting cradling cups of tea, chip papers stuffed into the waste bucket, the kids eating theirs next door in the bedsit, watching television.

'They're OK, Maggie, honest. He can't have talked to them for long, as soon as he saw me coming he cleared off quick. Probably they didn't see a thing, and if they did, well, they've both seen blokes in the bath before now —'

'Balls. They should bloody well have stuck around till we turned up. How were they to know we weren't kept late at work? They're the ones supposed to be looking after the kids in the day-time, they should bloody well make sure there aren't any funny characters hanging around outside —'

Jo sounds more aggressive than usual, which means she is worried.

Maggie calms down straight away, pats her arm and pours her another cup of tea.

'Ok, you're right, they don't really care that much. Got to get home to their old man, I daresay. That means we'll have to bloody well do something ourselves —'

'What, stop perverts hanging around? How —'

'No, you silly bugger, it's not just that. Well, I mean, it's the whole bloody mess. I don't know, maybe we ought to give up work. Or what we could do, well, what I mean-is, maybe wouldn't do any harm going down to the pub tonight to see if the others are there, only a quick drink mind, we can't be sure what they're like yet —'

'But they want to talk about work, Maggie, get us into a union and all that. They haven't got kids, I don't think, they don't know what it's like —'

'Well, they bloody should then, What's the use of going on about unions and higher pay and all that—we're still stuck with the nursery closing at half-past three. You tell me where there's a union'll get me a job that pays me any more to go off at half-past three —'

'I don't know, do I, course there bleeding isn't. And anyway, even if we ask them, I mean, even if they think we can do something about it, though Christ knows what, I don't want a lot of knowalls who haven't got any kids and don't know the first thing about them telling us what to do with ours —'

'Well, we won't let them, that's all,' Maggie says lamely. 'Anyway, no harm just going, you were going to go, you said so, it was you wanted a night out. Let's go and just have a drink, Ted'll look after the kids, your Lucy can sleep in Frieda's bed, be a bit of company for her.'

Jo and Maggie arm-in-arm down the street to the Railway Tavern, high heels clicking on the paving behind the packing sheds. The sun like a peach at seven, furring the railway lines with light. Shivering pleasantly in her new blouse trimmed with lace nicked from Silvex Modes the week before, two quid borrowed from Ted means they can afford a few halves, jumping over the gutter full of leaves.

Jo's feeling OK now, going out with Maggie, she's back to teasing.

'What about your programme, then, those Amazons?'

'Piss off, Ted'll watch it for me. Oh, no he won't, there's football on, the other side. Well, I don't know, probably wouldn't have been much good anyway —'

'What's made you change your mind?'

Joe isn't really interested, she's busy lighting her cigarette. Standing in the pub doorway out of the wind striking her third match, the goddess of beer depicted in glowing-coloured tiles on either side of her, massive arms holding up sheaves of grain. Pushing open the door of the pub. Gust of warmth, beer and music rushing out to meet them and suck them in towards the bar. On your own, darling? Come and join us then, patting her thigh. Fuck off, Steve, will you, I'm with my friend tonight. Two halves of bitter please, thanks, love. Sitting at a table in the corner so that they can see the door, catch the others' eyes when they come in. Maggie drawing pictures with her fingertips in the spilt beer on the marble tabletop.

'Those Amazons? Bit of a fairy tale really, isn't it, so what if there's still some around. See me with one of my tits cut off, can't you, just the excuse for Ted to be off after Betty Ash again—'

While they're still laughing the others arrive all at once. Shifting round the table, squashing up against Jo to make room for them all. The two women from the Charter are in jeans this time, a bit scruffy. None of us exactly Dave Whatsit's ideal woman, you could say. Maggie takes a sip of beer to remind the others that that's all she's there for, and looks defiantly around. No flies on us, we'll soon see what you're like.

The Right Hand on the Day of Judgement
Valerie Miner

'What do you think of that piece from Zaragoza?' Kathy asked. 'Will you give me the OK? Can we count on Tony to keep it quiet?'

'It's a dilemma, all right, something I've been weighing up all morning,' said Harry.

Kathy could never tell which was misshapen — Harry or the old gaberdine suit. A proper Charlie Chaplin, he was, with manilla envelopes and foolscap carbon sheets hanging from his creased brown leather briefcase. No, more of James Stewart as the absent-minded diplomat, bumbling through social banalities, but driven with political commitment. He hadn't bothered to comb the grey wisps over his baldness this morning. She wondered how old Harry was — somewhere in his late fifties if he had fought in Spain.

'Remember Tony's antics in Uruguay,' said Kathy, 'flaunting his press card. He was lucky to escape intact. We may be spending a lot of money for him to holiday in prison.'

'Yes, yes,' nodded Harry. 'Perhaps we *should* reconsider the assignment.'

She played with the coffee seed beads hanging to the waist of her black pullover. The seed beads — being cheap, a tribute to the Brazilian Liberation Fund and still stylish — were among her more successful compromises. She concentrated on Harry's careful words.

'On the other hand,' he watched her, 'one has to take certain risks, like we did last year over the invasion of Prague.'

She released the beads and picked up her fountain pen.

Harry continued, 'I suppose that's what journalistic courage is all about. To hell with it. Tell Tony to go ahead. I'll trust my instincts. By the way, thanks for finishing up the layouts. You're my right hand. Don't know what I would do without you.'

Kathy packed the solicitor's letters and her notes on South African sport into the frayed blue folder marked 'Mock-Up'. She listened to the muffled slam from the small front room. The office gulping another

person. She felt stuffy lately, cramped. She never believed those gas fires
were healthy.

Hilary rang the next day, at the worst possible time. And she was into
that damn consciousness raising trip. But she *was* funny, when she got
sarcastic about Harry. Kathy really wanted to laugh. Instead, she said,
'Nonsense, Hilary. He is totally committed to the struggle. This paper is
his life.'

'Then he better start making funeral arrangements,' said Hilary. 'If
The Artisan survives, it's *your* doing. You're responsible for organising
the mock-up, for convincing the contributors to stick around, for getting
Colson to reconsider publishing. You've resuscitated it.'

'Enough high drama,' said Kathy. 'Sometimes I wonder how much
you defend me just because I'm a woman. Anyway, *enough*, because I've
got to get back to work.'

'All right, kid. If things don't work out on TA, though, you know
you've always got a job back in Birmingham. Take care — of yourself.
Cheers!'

Kathy hung up and turned to the secretary,

'Alice, could you hold any calls for twenty minutes?'

She spoke through the pots of drugged ferns. She hated the gas fire. If
it did this to the plants, what did it do to the people? She stared past
Alice, through the dingy window panes. The brick wall across the alley
looked like the pointilism she had studied at the National Gallery last
term, the image alternately diffused and discernible. She had to clean
that window.

The flaccid blonde woman nodded politely from inside her *Daily Mail*,
looked up and smiled obligingly, 'OK Mrs . . . I mean, Kathy. I'll tell
them you're in a meeting.'

It had taken Alice six weeks to call her Kathy. But who was she to talk?
It had taken *her* four *months* to call Harry, Harry. (The same thing with
her mother-in-law. It would have been so much easier if she had said,
'Call me "Mum" or "Annabel" or "Mrs Edwards."') And he was
characteristically indifferent that day she finally got up the nerve to say,
'Harry, I think . . .'

'We should work on the logo and the pages if we're going to get them
in by Friday.'

'Yes, yes,' he said. 'And the solicitor's coming. Can you tie that up for
me? I've got some work to do on the censorship piece. Perhaps you could
come in after lunch?'

'Sure, Harry.'

She got a good start and didn't want to break for lunch. When people
asked why she worked so hard she explained that in a dotty way, she
believed in *The Artisan*. 'Britain's radical literary forum.' Their coverage

of the Indo-China War was closely watched. She was proudest of the space they gave to trades union politics, to non-intellectuals, breaking down media elitism. She felt like she was helping to change things, not directly, but by being a resource for people who could.

Harry didn't buzz her that afternoon. Just as well because she worked into the evening with the editing. Harry hated multiple reviews, but she was glad she had suggested juxtaposing the books on Canadian and Irish autonomy. Anyway, he would like the critique of *The Female Eunuch*. This chap showed how women's liberation was a bourgeois deviation from the class struggle. If they continued all this nitpicking about who ran meetings, nothing would get done. Hilary would scream Left chauvinism, but Kathy agreed with the article. What was wrong with complimenting a man's work at home or in the office, if it were all part of the *same* struggle. What was wrong with typing, for instance? It had been her entree into university politics where she met Craig and into TA itself.

The telephone echoed in the empty room. She hesitated, not wanting to go home late again.

'Senior Harry Simpson, por favor.'

'I'm sorry,' she scrambled for her A level Espagnol. 'Senor Simpson no esta aqui.'

'Oh, Kathy,' an English voice broke in. 'I'm glad I caught *you*.' The operator faded in a garble of Spanish. 'This is Tony Smythe. I've got a great lead. Marquez is briefing a few journalists in the hills above Zaragoza. I need more money and time if I'm going to cover it.'

'I'll get Harry on the phone tonight and we'll settle . . .'

'No, no time for that. The MULA are taking a small group of us into the hills. They're leaving in an hour. I need to know right away whether I can have £100 expenses and four days on the deadline. If I don't leave with them this evening, I'll never get into the camp.'

'Give me forty-five minutes to reach Harry.'

'Forty.'

'Right, ring me back in forty minutes.'

How could Harry refuse an exclusive briefing with Marquez . . . the number was engaged . . . but then, Harry was so reticent about 'untested' revolutionaries. Kathy dialled the number again. Engaged. And again. She would never make it over to Albany Street and back in forty minutes. But Craig could. Her only option was to ring Craig.

'Kathy, love, where the hell are you?'

'I'm afraid I'm still at work. Something has come up. An emergency call from Spain. Tony has a chance to go to Marquez' camp, but we have to reach him with the OK in thirty-five minutes.' (Silence from the other end of the line.) 'I'll explain later. Could you do me a huge favour? I can't get Harry on the phone. Could you drive over there and tell him to ring me here?'

'Well, I don't know. I have my doubts about the Marquez position.
The caucus was just discussing how that kind of nationalism . . .

'Oh, come on, Craig. At least the story should be covered. You can't
ignore a movement as large as that.'

'Fucking hell, it's not as if I don't have enough to do, preparing the
caucus platform, finding time to do my thesis.'

'Craig, look, I'm sorry to impose. Dear, *I'm sorry* I'm late again. But
this could mean the survival of TA.'

'What about the survival of something euphemistically known as our
marriage?'

She agreed with Craig's belief in 'healthy confrontation,' but she just
didn't have time right now.

'Craig, you're being unfair. Let's talk about this when I get home.
Please drive over to Harry's.' The authority in her voice seemed to
support her and restrain him. 'Ask him to ring me on the 07 line.'

When she hung up the only remorse she felt was from her Yoga teacher's
lectures on back tension. How *could* she have taken from Craig's abuse
this long? His rambling accusations as he peered into the aquarium
feeding his Black Bullheads and Veiltails. The phone rang and she
answered it with relief.

'Kathy? Harry here. What's all this about a Spanish Revolution?'

She quickly recounted the story.

'I'll have to think about it.'

'But that's the problem. There's no *time* to think about it. Tony is
calling back in twenty minutes.'

'Why did you arrange a fool thing like that? This is a big decision. We
risk a huge feature hole. On the other hand, a good piece could swing
Colson's judgment.'

'Yes, yes,' she said not meaning to be so brusque, 'however, we've *got*
to make a decision.'

'Don't pressure me,' he said. 'I'll ring you back.'

'OK, Harry, but please remember to call within fifteen minutes.'

'I did hear you the first time. Good-bye.'

Had she been too dogged? Craig always said she got hyper in
emergencies. Better that than Harry's paralysis. Three minutes to nine.
She started to ring Harry, then realised she had to leave the other line
open. TA's survival could be secured with one good story. She tried to get
Harry on 06 before Tony called back. The number was engaged.
Mollified she thought Harry must be ringing back, but no, no, of course
not. The other line was still. What the hell was he doing?

She put down the receiver. Immediately, it rang.

'Go ahead with it, Tony. Where do you want the money wired?'

She noted the details of his itinerary and gave him three, not four, extra days for the deadline. She felt elated, surprised at her confidence and her indifference to Harry. She put on her raincoat and gathered several articles into her briefcase. He could call her at home if he wanted to find out what had happened.

Kathy walked briskly to the bus-stop. Usually she let herself be sucked home on the tube. She hated the way people in the underground corridors rushed unconsciously past each other, like numbers in the formula of an ironic computer programmer. The tube was part of her mindless survival in London. (By the time she shuffled to get a smoking compartment, jostled to find a seat, arranged her briefcase and groceries on her lap, she was too exhausted to do anything but close her eyes, practise her Yoga breathing and hope to exhale the parentheses with which she had ordered the day.) Tonight, she saw a 137 as soon as she turned the corner. She clinked two-and-a-half pence in the newsvendor's tin, picked up an *Evening Standard* and hailed the swaggering wagon.

Kathy climbed to the top of the bus. She still saw London as a visitor. The Thames from Chelsea Bridge. 'Girls, this is the Thames, the mighty river down which Julius Caesar and Saint Ardith journeyed,' explained Sister Margaret on that Easter expedition to London. St Ardith was the patron of their order. Kathy had been chagrined last month to hear that St Ardie as the girls in the dining hall called her, had been checked off the rolls. Even though Kathy had stopped attending Mass five years ago, she felt betrayed by St Ardie. She studied the floodlit Palace of Westminster, so absurdly elegant for a Labour Government. Westminster Abbey curtsied like a venerable chatelaine in dust-starched skirts. The bus swung around murky Hyde Park Corner, then through the harsh fluorescence of Oxford Street. As they rode up to Camden Town, she turned to her newspaper. She couldn't concentrate on *Two-Tiered Health Service, Israel Rejects Amnesty* or *Neigh on EEC Farm Policy*. She opted out for a curious feature about an American vicar who wanted to father a child. His wife was infertile, so he offered £4,000 for a woman with the proper genetic components to be artificially inseminated and to bear him a baby. 'Rent-a-body,' thought Kathy. Hilary would call this exploitative. The bus was waddling up towards Archway, so she folded the paper under her arm and manoeuvred down the steps.

Craig wasn't home. He probably stopped off at the pub after Harry's. She just wanted to forget the whole mess. So she tidied up the living-room and went into the kitchen to make Craig's sandwiches. She always made them at night because she hated the smell of mustard in the morning. She left him a sweet note before crawling under the duvet. The shadow of his body became noticeable in the first light. She hadn't heard him come back. She must have slept well. She left him undisturbed at 6 a.m.

'Mr Simpson had to leave for Scotland unexpectedly,' Alice said quickly. 'He told me that I was to refer any calls to you. He said you would understand about the Scottish piece, interviewing Mr Wolfe and all. He said he would ring you.'

She didn't understand and he didn't ring. Her anxiety about the Marquez piece disappeared in the havoc of a dozen other decisions about the type and photographs and cartoons. She didn't have time to panic. Occasionally she would notice herself taking action and review her decision peripherally. She was afraid that if she acknowledged her authority too directly, she might . . . actually she didn't know just what she was afraid of.

The Greer review still bothered her. Somehow it wasn't conclusive enough. She knew before she made the phone call that she shouldn't ask Hilary for advice.

Hilary exploded, 'Sure, sure there are a lot of problems with ''feminist analysis'', but Greer doesn't represent the whole Women's Movement. Just like every black prick doesn't represent African liberation.'

'Oh, come on, Hilary. You can't possibly equate the oppression of women to the exploitation of the Third World. That really is going too far.' She was almost shouting down the line. 'Look, I've got to get back to work.'

The last two days accelerated with the pressure of deadline against Harry's loose subbing. She grew more and more annoyed with him and then realised it wasn't fair. Harry was just distracted. Normally he was a great editor and the most *political* person she knew. He had gone through so much with the Communist Party in the 50s, no wonder he was a bit threadbare.

When he ambled into the office on Monday, Kathy settled for a modest admonition. 'Harry, you know I had to make a decision about the Marquez piece.'

'The Marquez . . . oh, yes. I think I tried to ring you back, but I was interrupted. Then Ethel made some emergency call. Sorry about that. I reckoned you were perfectly sensible. What did you tell him?'

'To take three extra days for the story. I wired £100 expenses.'

'That's fine,' he said as he walked into his office. He stuck his head back around the door. 'Oh, I do have some questions about those columns in the front of the paper. The multiple review. I've told you before that this isn't an academic journal. I suppose it's too late now. Could you stop by the office on the way back from the printer's tonight? I'd like to talk over that promotion with you.'

'I'm sorry, Harry, but I promised Craig a real supper tonight. It's our fifth|anniversary.' She tried to rationalise the sentimentality, but before she could come up with something that might satisfy Harry, he said,

'Neither of us will be able to afford supper if this mock-up isn't approved. Come on. I promise to give you a couple of days off at the end of this thing.'

Damn. She thought she wasn't some functionary scurrying after a Christmas bonus. What did he think she was doing while he was in Scotland? Hang on. She would sound like Hilary in a minute. Hang on. The promotion *did* have to be done. Watch the bourgeois individualism. Hang on, Kathy.

They met for two hours that evening and she briefed him on last week's decisions. He reassured her that she had done as well as he could have done.

Craig was furious. He was having a hard enough time doing his research lately. When he borrowed time to spend with her she could at least respect his schedule. As far as he could see, she was *always* having emergencies and he wondered — just wondered without being too analytical about it — how many of them were escapes from their shitty relationship. Since she didn't seem to find the occasion so portentous, he felt free to study and would return when dinner was ready. He wished her Happy Anniversary, by the way.

Salad making always soothed her. When she was little, the loveliest thing about getting married was going to be sitting in a blue tiled kitchen reaching into the cornucopia for another cucumber. She liked to score the cucumbers on the edges with a fork so that when she cut them they came out as unpredictably as paper dolls. (She and Craig were the best of their generation, the archetypal virile revolutionaries who might be photographed for marijuana advertisements in a few years. Bright. Confident, committed. He would finish his Ph.D. in psychology and they would take up his post in Havana. She would raise their kids in a healthy workers' state. But the order seemed to be breaking down. Kathy wasn't sure she wanted to quit her job. Craig let his thesis drag on another year. He never did anything overt to annoy her — that's why she felt it was her fault — it was what he didn't do. She couldn't count on him for anything. In the end, he didn't even do his own work. Maybe she put too much pressure on him.) Tomatoes were satisfying. If they were firm and fresh. She hated the over-ripe ones that sagged under the knife and squirted messily over the glistening chopping board. Raw mushrooms were best, falling into thin porous slices like wafers of fungus. The lettuce could be tedious when it was too wet. (She felt like a real bitch sometimes. She had to pry to learn what happened during his day. The conversation would be like an oral exam with halting, circumspect replies. Sometimes his withdrawal was an ambush. Like that weekend of the Third World Medical Conference. He insisted he wanted to go. Then on Thursday he announced that he still hadn't fixed the thermostats in the monkey room — Thursday! Her work schedule was ruined for two weeks. It was only afterwards she realised she might have gone alone.) Kathy carefully dried the leaves until they looked like a heavy green tissue paper she used for collages when she was a child. Fun, all this cutting and reassembling. That's what she liked best — putting it all in order. She detested random salads — crisp stews in smudged glass bowls. First, she put in the bits of lettuce, then the celery, onion, mushrooms. She sprinkled rosemary and basil. On top she wheeled the tomatoes and the cucumbers. (Craig would understand once they had a chance to sit down and discuss the chaos at work. To be fair, she hadn't told him very much. She always got home so late. After the supper and the cleaning and the news, there was no time to talk.) The chops were sizzling and the potatoes were done just the way he liked them, with the jackets falling off.

'Craig,' she called into the livingroom. 'Craig.'

No answer, so she set the hotplates on the stove and looked in. 'Craig,' she said gently. He was asleep at his desk, his head on a new Asimov science fiction book. 'Craig,' she said compassionately. This petulant boy was her protector and partner for life? 'Craig,' she said bitterly. She couldn't cope with the anger; she didn't know where to release it — at him — or at her own poor judgement. This is our anniversary, she told herself. She thought about the layouts she had to do tonight. She shook him. 'Harry,' she said and stopped. How often she almost had said that. It was eerie. How often she had mixed them up in dreams. And once, when she had promised Craig to deposit his grant in his chequeing account, she had put it in Harry's instead. She felt like such an idiot when the cashier showed her the numbers were different.

Craig looked up. '*Who* did you call?'

'Sorry, love. I'm always incoherent when I'm tired.'

'Well, *I*'m too tired to indulge myself right now. I think I'll go off to a proper bed.'

'But you haven't eaten. And it's our anniversary.'

'I suppose you should have thought about both those items a little earlier. I'm worn out. See you in the morning.' He stumbled up from the swivel chair, almost knocking over the half-empty bottle of sherry. She hungrily regarded the level, a sufficient ablution for guilt. She was grateful they still shared something.

Kathy awoke late with a terrible hangover. Not so much an alcoholic headache as a residue of remorse. She rose immediately, careful not to awaken Craig. She saw herself gazing into a cup of black coffee. Running to the tube. Answering the phones. What was she doing in London, her life was as illusory as St Ardie's.

'Hello, Kathy? This is Hilary. Got a news bulletin for you. Colson is coming down. Thought I should warn you that I got carried away with him yesterday. He was expounding on the vigour and genius of one Harry Simpson.'

Kathy didn't say anything, too afraid to think what Hilary had said *for* her.

'Well, you know, kid, I'm not utterly indiscreet. I didn't let on that Harry was an absolute moron.'

Kathy didn't know what bothered her more — Harry's fraudulence or her own complicity. Just how long did she think she could continue playing the innocent minion.

'What did you say to Colson?' she asked tentatively.

'Not much — I just dropped a few hints about Harry's long sojourns away from the office and his banker's hours. I reckoned the rest was up to you.'

Kathy rang off and buzzed Harry's office. 'Harry, I've got to talk to you.'

'Sure, sure,' he muttered. 'And would you bring in those readership surveys. Also the circulation reports. Colson has decided to catch us off guard. This could mean the end of TA if we're not prepared.'

She watched him take notes on her work. He tried, at first, to comprehend, but by one o'clock he was just grasping for details, for a semblance of competence. Harry hadn't made a straightforward judgement in months. What appeared to be his preoccupation with deadline was simply failed nerve. She had always responded discreetly, making her decisions sound like clerical minutiae. At the end of the day she told Harry that she wanted to be in on the conference. He was surprised, then agreed with alacrity. Of course, of course, it was a *sensible* idea.

The next morning, the fragrant and glossy mock-up arrived an hour before Colson was due. Kathy was proud of it all — the classic logo, the solid articles, the lively layout. It was so perfectly formed. She was as amazed and satisfied as Mary had been with her baby. And after last night, she might have to resign herself to this kind of posterity. She and Craig had never had such a row. It was more like a schism although it was just about the familiar issues — him charging that she spent too much time at work; her retorting that he felt jealous because he couldn't do his own work. He said she was a real career woman, all right, more career than woman. He told her she would have to make a choice, decide what she wanted. Kathy surprised both of them by saying she didn't know what she wanted and went to bed. Now, she looked forward to Colson's visit so much that she could hardly concentrate on the circulation figures.

Harry buzzed her on the intercom. 'Great. Great. Just what I imagined. I really couldn't have done it without you.'

What could you expect from Harry?

In the middle of the morning, a heavily cologned man in a grey striped suit and a thin paisley tie lumbered up to her.

'Harry Simpson, please,' he blustered, his hand leaning heavily on her desk.

Before she had time to explain that Harry Simpson had a meeting this morning, the man added,

'My name is Colson, Carl Colson. I think Harry's expecting me.' He pulled a wrinkled beige handkerchief from his back pocket and wiped his forehead. 'Terrible stairs. Ever think of getting a lift installed?'

This was the visionary publisher they had been struggling to impress for two months? This was the man whose judgement would determine their jobs and the fate of *The Artisan*? She hadn't expected Leon Trotsky, but . . .

'Just one moment, please,' she heard herself assuming the grace she had expected of him. How hollow did her voice sound? How contemptuous was her face? She watched him thanking her, taking a chair, smiling at her. She supposed she was smiling at him.

'Carl, Carl, welcome.' Harry thrust his hand into the pudgy mitt of Carl Colson. '*Sorry*, I had *no* idea you were waiting. How long have they kept you here?' He ushered him inside. She waited demurely for her invitation, but Harry didn't even turn around to nod before he shut the door.

'Well, well,' she heard him say to Colson. 'What do you think of my baby? How about the logo, eh?'

She couldn't endure the thought of them sitting in the large office congratulating each other. She went out to the loo to wash her face. When she came back, she was still flushed and her copy of the magazine was gone.

'They've taken it in,' said Alice delicately. 'They said they didn't want anything to happen to it.'

What goddam arrogance. It was her sweat, her work. What absolute nerve!

She heard the intercom buzz.

Perhaps she had been too rash. Perhaps they had just expected her to follow them in. Perhaps she should just go in now and save the formality of answering the line. No, she would wait for them to ask her. She deserved that much.

'Kathy, I was wondering if you could do us a favour?'

'Sure, I'll be right in.'

'No need to trouble yourself. Could you just ask Alice — her line seems to be broken — could you just ask Alice to bring us two cups of sugared tea?'

'Sure, Harry. Sure.'

She rotely relayed the message and watched Alice prepare the tea, place it on the tray with some digestives and take it in. Suddenly, Kathy felt nothing but the pure release of acrimony. She was too angry to be intimidated, too angry for judgement. Kathy got up and banged on the door.

She was greeted by an astonished Alice, carrying an empty tray in one hand and a stack of file folders in the other. Kathy smiled and quickly walked past into the office.

'I've finished that work, Harry. I can come in now.'

'Yes, yes, Mrs Edwards,' expanded Colson. 'Do come in. Harry tells me you're such a bright girl, with drive and personality.' Colson brightened, 'Harry says you're his right hand.'

'Sorry to inform you about the amputation.'

'I beg your pardon?' asked Colson.

'This girl's got a great sense of humour, Carl, just one of the things I haven't told you about her.' Harry smiled indulgently. When Kathy didn't smile back, Harry stuttered for a transition.

Kathy interceded. 'I'm thinking about leaving the paper, going back to a job in Birmingham, unless some important changes are made.'

Harry sat still.

'But, but,' sputtered Colson. 'This is a silly time for that, my love. I mean, just when *The Artisan* has been reborn. This mock-up is brilliant. And to think we were all so afraid of failure.'

'And of success.'

'What was that, my dear?'

'Listen, this is a good start, but only that. We could have much more direct reporting from South America and Africa, a broader review policy.' She knew she wasn't talking to either of them, but enjoying the rush of her own ideas. 'A wider circulation in the North, some hard investigative pieces — like a series on multinationals.'

'That's all very well, but hang on, girl, and look at what Harry's done for a moment. The multiple review is superb; the Marquez piece is a real coup.'

She had no reason to expose Harry now. He and Colson could find out about each *other*. 'Look, I'll outline the ideas. You can think about them. If you agree, I'll stay and help. If you don't, I've got another job waiting. I suppose political commitment is portable.'

They turned to Harry. 'Yes,' he said wearily, 'they sound like good ideas. Perhaps we could discuss them after lunch?'

'Well, well,' said Colson brightly, glancing quickly at his watch, 'of course we're open to change. Just look at this issue. The mark of a real revolutionary editor.'

'I know,' said Kathy, retrieving her copy and walking out of the office.

Just Lie Back and Think of the Empire
Michele Roberts

The airport at Singapore is like any other except that it is filled with white men wearing long shorts. The East starts here.

The air hostesses on the flight to Bangkok wear pink and purple sarongs with gold borders, western eye-makeup, smiles. They bow gracefully to all the passengers, catching the men's eyes with a practised coquetry that yet seems charmingly fresh, then vanish backwards with tiny steps to reappear with hot towels and orchid sprays. As the plane hangs in darkness over a net of lights far below, Kate looks in amazement at her new sandals and the label on her hand luggage. Her stomach lurching in sympathy with the plane dropping down fast towards Bangkok convinces her dully that it's she who's done it: left England, friends, comrades, ways of seeing, the easy labels of self-definition. Miss Bourgeois Individualist of the 1970s, vital statistics a BA in Eng. Lit. and a diploma in librarianship, and a deep interest in people and travel.

Kate's local women's group gives her a farewell party of disapproval veiled by loyalty. A basement room in a north London squat, wild and bright with plants, hangings covering the crumbled plaster falling off the damp walls, furnished with wit and ingenuity by dint of jumble sales and the skips outside the richer homes further down the street. Her friends' comments are on the level of rhetoric; no-one can speak on the personal level of hurt.

'I don't see why you're going,' Annie says, sprawled out on the bed on the floor, 'when there's so much beginning to happen here.' Swinging her boots up on to the Indian bedspread to indicate her lack of concern.

Pat, who is always totally commited to every idea and action she enters, underlines the certainty of her words with a hand stabbing a cigarette into a saucer serving as ashtray.

'You don't need to go and work as a librarian abroad, for God's sake. Dishing out British Government aid, what a cop-out. There's all those women talking about setting up a feminist information centre, they need people to help, you're trained for it, and here you are going away —'

Ex-Catholic Jean states flatly, 'You ought to stay.'

'You're so moral about it,' Kate complains, uneasy at the unspoken attack beneath the supposedly supportive criticism, 'correct, incorrect —'

'Come on,' Annie drawls, glinting over her glass of beer, 'stop avoiding the issue, will you? We're asking you — why the British Committee? Why Thailand?'

In preparation for this moment and its resulting confusion in her head Kate has a speech ready which she repeats selfconsciously, aware of how pompous she sounds but not why.

'I want to test one set of certainties by opposing them to another. I don't know, I want to find out if I do really believe what I say I do and if I want the kind of life I say I do, and the only way to do that seems to be to get right away and try a straight career for a bit, just to see how I react.'

'Sounds as though you're the one being moral now,' Jean says drily. 'You make feminism sound like a set of philosophical opinions. And what's all this purist stuff about straight careers?'

'It's so bloody elitist,' complains Annie through a mouthful of salami. 'You take off to the other side of the world to get a clearer perspective on what's happening here, right? You put yourself into cold storage for two years as far as any kind of political practice goes and just sit and think — and don't forget you'll get paid £5000 a year to sit and think about the purity of the struggle we're all fighting back here.'

'I think you're being unfair,' Kate says, unable to respond directly to the criticism and so simply feeling hurt. 'I'm only trying to work things out for myself and take a bit of responsibility for what I do.'

'For God's sake,' Pat interposes, 'do you suppose that that isn't what we're all trying to do? Work out the relation between feminism and our own personal practice and our wider political practice? I think you're just running away from the difficulties that that entails. Isn't that the real reason? That you see the struggle as demanding too much from you personally and so you want to get right away from it for a while?'

'Well,' Annie says calmly, 'if that is the real reason, Kate, why can't you admit it?'

'Because all I can ever do is bloody leave — one group after another. I don't know what's wrong with me —' Kate mutters, nearly in tears.

Mary, who has said nothing up until now, stirs in her seat in the corner of the room. 'Kate, lots of us are in that confusion, honestly. And if different women are at different places to start working from, that's a fact, not a put-down, you don't have to feel guilty about it.'

'I'm not going to Thailand just to escape from the group,' Kate says, still unable to move away from guilt. 'There are other things involved —'

Jean interrupts her before she has a chance to fumble into what those things are.

'Yes. Like you said. Self-discovery and all that. Much pleasanter when you can get a suntan while you're doing it.'

'What I don't see,' Pat says, interposing kindly from her belief that Kate is incapable of replying, 'is why you have to go so far. Why go to the extreme of joining the British Committee for Christ's sake?'

'I haven't got the money just to go as a traveller, and there aren't that many jobs abroad. I applied for several and this one came up, that's all, I didn't choose it particularly.'

'Why not?' says Annie, flicking an olive pip into Kate's lap, 'why the hell not choose and make decisions if you're in a position where you can? It doesn't necessarily mean being totally idealistic — there are some situations where you can take control —'

Kate's stomach feels out of control. She has felt sick ever since the final board interview: four middleaged middle-class men rub their hands at her qualifications, her feminine ability to spot what they want her to say and to say it, her freaky clothes that suggest her safe token Marxism and her fashionably feminist views. She knows from the start she will get the job and participates with passive fascination in the necessary motions; the selection board chivalrously closes the door on the trap she has set herself. She signs a contract, is given a generous clothes and household goods allowance. Till death do us part.

The one promise that Ben can't exact from her now. Two years of silence, of splits between her life with him and her commitment to politics desperately ended by leaving both. No way, she felt, of changing things with him, she was just there with him, he told her he loved her so there she was, identified and placed by the words he spoke of her. She'd come into the women's group after the others had spent some time talking about their individual relations to femaleness; feminism for her was a safe place, a rhetoric spoken to her by other women, a description they made of her, a set of ideas they had worked out and which she acquired to wear as a badge. As a result, for her the only way to struggle with men was to run, as far away as possible. She had no words of her own; independence, selfhood, meant travelling on her own.

As Kate steps off the plane the heat passes in fierce waves across her face, gagging her like another wet towel.

She is expecting to be met by a local member of Committee staff and so is not surprised when a young Thai dressed formally in dark trousers and white short-sleeved shirt and carrying a dark peaked cap comes up to her and says, 'Excuse me, you are waiting for some-one?'

'Yes,' she replies eagerly, 'someone from the British Committee is supposed to be meeting me.'

'Fine, fine,' he says, 'please come with me.'

He picks up her suitcases and heads for the exit. The night is black and humid; sweat crawls under her armpits, between her thighs on the plastic-covered seat, courses between her breasts. They are bumping along a wide highway, stalls stacked with water melons separating the two streams of traffic, the outlines of corrugated-iron roofs defining a shantytown on either side. Her escort lounges in the driving seat, one hand laid casually on the wheel, the other engaged in smoothing back his hair in a relaxed manner belied by the slightly puzzled looks he flicks sideways at her. He fires questions at her.

'You had a good trip? You are hot? You like it here? My name is Sadat. You want some Coke? There is a crate in the back.'

She reaches over into the back and grabs a couple of cans from the crate lying on the back seat next to his peaked cap. Noticing that her hands are shaking and knowing that he has noticed she forces herself to act cool, not daring for the moment to analyse her disquiet lest she is incapable of handling the reason. Carry on the way you're going, pretend it's not happening, lie back and relax, just keep quiet and it'll be all right in the end, urges the female chorus in her stomach.

She smiles brightly at her companion and enquires:

'How long have you been in this job?'

He frowns and stares straight ahead, blows a furious klaxon on the horn. The car leaps forward, tears between two lorries and lurches back into the middle lane.

'This job? Several years now. I hope for promotion soon to Chief Steward. And you? What's your name? What do you do here?'

Panic kickstarts her stomach. She fumbles for defusing words.

'But I thought — surely you know my name? Didn't they tell you that when they sent you to collect me?'

'Sanay tell me how you look. But he no tell me your name.'

She forces it out.

'I don't understand. Where are we going? Which hotel did they tell you to drive me to?'

Sadat turns a face of smooth surprise to her, hands still controlling expertly wheels and gears.

'I no know which hotel you go to. Maybe the Asia, maybe the Atlanta. Sanay just ask me to drive you into town, baby.'

'You mean you're not from the British Committee? I thought—'

Sadat gazes at her coolly.

'But why you no say so before, baby? You mean you not Sanay's girlfriend? But we drive fourteen kilometres now and you not say —'

She clutches her can of Coke and pinpoints her collusion in what her insides scream is her kidnapping. The cap on the back seat beside the crate of Coke bears a badge plainly reading Siam Intercontinental. How long has she known Sadat could not possibly be a British Committee driver? Once more she tries to force herself out of passively accepting an alienating situation out of terror.

'There's been a mistake. You must drive me back to the airport. Perhaps the people who came to meet me will still be there —' She smiles desperately at him, her insides shaking with fantasies of what will happen if he refuses.

Obediently, resignedly, he swings the car round in a dangerous U-turn at the next intersection and they flash back towards the airport, the jewel factories and towerblocks of the Bangkok suburbs thinning out again to the dim outlines of swampy fields pierced by palmtree plantations. She is unable to gauge his mood, her feminine antennae have folded for the night. One act or speech is as arbitrary as another, being in the wrong car with the wrong man is in no way stranger than being in the wrong country in the wrong job. The sudden perception of the latter fact shatters her tenuous control; she concentrates for the moment on the former, blurting:

'I'm terribly sorry, I thought you were from the British Committee. At the airport you said —'

'British Committee? What is British Committee?'

She suppresses a hysterical giggle.

'You must know who they are. You know, a bit like the British Embassy, or-er-like USAID —'

'Ah; like USAID. You will stay here long time?'

Back to polite introductions. He blocks any attempt she makes to discover his role or intentions in all this. For the moment he is playing man about town to her confused tourist. She replies with suitable inanity.

'I'm here on a two-year contract. You speak very good English.'

A chink is temporarily exposed. He smiles to himself in the mirror.

'It's for the job,' he says proudly, 'I get promotion if I speak good English.'

They swing in at the airport gates. Not a light in any of the lounges or offices, not a soul, certainly not a British Committee one, who looks like a welcoming committee. The one security guard patrolling Arrivals does not speak English. Kate drags back to the carpark. Sadat is suddenly redefined as her only friend.

'Could we try the British Embassy, d'you think? They'd have the Committee's address, at least. Or perhaps I should just wait here — perhaps someone's gone into town to look for me and will come back eventually —'

Sadat shakes his head. 'You can't stay here, baby. They want to lock up now. No more planes. Besides, foreign girl can't stay here alone.'

She hesitates, gives in to his apparent grasp of possibilities. 'All right, let's go back into town. Would you drive me to the British Embassy?'

He acknowledges her humiliation by jumping out of his side of the car, coming round to hers, opening the door for her and waiting ostentatiously for her awkwardly to tuck her legs inside before closing it with a little bow. The comforting knowledge that at least she will get as far as the British Embassy tonight gives her the strength for attack.

'Whom did you say you were supposed to be meeting at the airport? Where d'you think she's got to? Shouldn't you go and look for her —?'

He turns his head and smiles. 'I think you her, baby. No difference now.'

She sits in silence for the rest of the drive. She begins to realise that he is bound to win, he is playing her in with an eternity of patience, amused and confident, indulging her now increases later enjoyment. I can't help it, Annie, I didn't choose to have this happen to me. Ben sighing in bed and talking to the pillow. Sorry, Kate. What can I do to give you an orgasm?

The Embassy is locked, shuttered, barred. Sadat lights a cigarette, with the engine still running, and watches the earnest set of Kate's back as she talks through the gates to the guard just inside. The tone of her voice has risen, she pushes the hair off her face with one worried hand while gesticulating with the other. Even from the kerb in the gloom the guard's shrugs and humorously uplifted eyes are visible as he declines to telephone the duty officer, ring a British Committee office empty at this time of night, break the sacred sleep of anyone else on the telephone list.

Sadat pitches his cigarette end through the window, gets out of the car and strolls to the gate. He speaks a few sentences of rapid Thai to the guard, who stares at the two of them, breaks into a comprehending smile and turns away back to his hut at the foot of the drive.

'Come on, baby,' says Sadat, managing to convey a weary but still kindly patience, 'he cannot help. I take you to hotel.'

'What did you say to him?' Kate demands, and then, as he refuses to hear, meekly amends this to 'Which hotel are you taking me to?'

'We try the Asia,' he says, 'though probably full, this time of night.'

With an increase of bland courtesy he insists that she stay in the car while he talks to the girl behind the Reception desk. The Asia is full up. Six hotels later she gives in.

'Look, couldn't you just lend me some Thai money? I could just walk around till morning and then go to the Committee office first thing—'

He turns a reproachful face on her for admitting what kind of a girl she is.

'You can't do that. You get into trouble. Only bad women on streets at night. No. We go to friend of mine who has motel.'

Giving her little time to question this version of the truth, he swings the car off the main road all concrete and glass buildings and turns down a tiny side street. Immediately the tarmac is soft and muddy, brown water gutters between the road and the wood and corrugated iron houses on each side, there are far fewer lights, open shop fronts are also cheap eating places and tiny spaces for sleeping. The car noses confidently down alley after alley. Now canals slap on either side, brimming with garbage and dead wood, an old man sleeps in an oilcan next to a garishly decorated lorry, men in vests and wide trousers, grouped playing cards by the light of oil lamps, raise their heads as the car's headlights sweep into their precarious privacy, and stare at her. Those eyes, sombre and steady yet lacking in curiosity, comfort her; they seem to know her, who she is, where she is going.

This definition is clarified when Sadat turns off the road through an entrance discreet enough to admit the car with only a centimetre on either side. They are in a smallish courtyard with parking space for perhaps half a dozen cars. All the lots are unoccupied, or so she thinks until a pair of green plastic curtains suddenly swishes around the car, enfolding them in a cave of green plastic gloom and she becomes aware of other cars and bodies breathing behind green silences.

'OK, here we are,' Sadat says unnecessarily, and pulls his bag off the back seat and gets out of the car. Just behind the car a small gap in the curtains reveals a door which leads into the motel apartment.

Kate puts her suitcase down on a green plastic-covered pouffe and gapes. Green plastic quilting pads the walls, an enormous mirror on the ceiling reflects a similarly-sized double bed. One wall is see-through glass to the lavatory with more green furnishings. A bible by the bed is the gift of the Gideon Missionary Society.

Sadat opens his airline holdall and produces a bottle of Moet-Chandon, deftly flips off the cork and pours a golden stream into two plastic toothmugs.

'I thought maybe I go to a party,' he explains, 'so I bring bottle from aeroplane. My friends wait for me now but never mind.'

He hands her a beaker of champagne. She sits on the edge of the bed, takes a sip, catches sight of her knees in the mirror overhead and remembers her prepared speech.

'Look, it's terribly kind of you to find me a place to stay, but you must let me give you the money. I mean, you needn't really have bothered with looking after me.'

He disagrees with the version of events contained in this last sentence by ignoring it and saying smilingly, 'You no pay here, baby. Manager is friend of mine. I have key.'

Forced on to what she really meant to say, Kate fumbles for words, absurdly feeling she has to simplify, patronise in order for him to understand her in a language foreign to him, that she must not hurt his feelings, he is part of the oppressed majority, colonised daily by the people she has come to work for.

'Look, you've been really kind to me. I mean, we're friends now, aren't we? But you've got to understand — I'm not going to sleep with you. I'm terribly grateful to you for all your help, but we'll just be friends tonight, OK?'

From what depths of unease and powerlessness emerges all this gratitude desperately proffered as pay for services not rendered? He has picked her up, lied to her, manipulated her insecurity and ignorance, and she is asking forgiveness for her lack of appreciation. He finishes the last of the champagne, stands up, smiles kindly at her.

'Sure, baby. Come on, we go to bed now.'

His body is slender, lean, brown, his prick a mere button at the top of his thighs. By contrast her body feels to her viewing it through his eyes overwhite, overlarge, overfloppy. She climbs onto the bed and lies six feet away from him. He turns onto his side, looks her up and down and says politely, 'What a beautiful shape.'

Visions of white blancmange released from a mould and failing to stand up invade her brain. She smiles awkwardly, suddenly hating herself yet wanting to placate him. 'Goodnight,' she says firmly and turns over on her side.

He moves in fast from behind, his prick starting lightning between her buttocks like a fork into sausage.

'Baby, I can make you very happy,' his voice pleads into her shoulder blades. She is now cockteasing bitch, he sensitive, easily hurt suitor. She inches to the edge of the bed, he follows; she lies on her back, his hand attempts to part her furiously dry lips; she wraps herself in the sheet, the tense warmth of his body suffocates her doubly; she leaps up and goes to the lavatory, he watches her through the glass wall.

Better get it over with, her mind urges her exhausted body, then at least you'll get a couple of hours sleep before dawn.

I offered no violence, officer, she didn't struggle, there are no marks on her body. She wasn't a virgin anyway, she must have wanted it really.

Confronted with his certainty so much stronger than her own, disorientation and alienation defusing lack of desire, she gives in as she has done before. She lies on her back, her feeling of deadness and detachment increased by watching the reflection in the overhead mirror like a television screen. She sees his narrow back move up and down, there is a vague irritation in her vagina, she watches his mouth move across her shoulders and face. Eventually he falls asleep, one arm outflung across her breasts so that she does not dare move it for fear of waking him, and, constricted, cannot sleep herself.

In the morning he is brisk, satisfied, picks up the room telephone and orders coffee for her. He collects it from the door when it arrives to spare her the embarrassment of being seen by the boy. He sits on the edge of the bed where Kate lies fenced in by bolsters and proffers it smilingly. The coffee is strong and sweet with a glass of tea accompanying it to drown the sweetness.

'You know any Thai?' he asks.

'No,' Kate says apologetically, 'they said I didn't need to bother to learn any before I came.'

'I teach you,' he says, 'say after me.'

Kate learns to say, 'I hate the Vietcong, I love the King and Queen' and 'One, two, three' by the time breakfast is over. She glances at her watch. Unease returns to shatter her friendly complicity and she jumps up.

'It's half past eight. I ought to go — the office must open around nine.'

She stands beyond the see-through wall and grimaces to herself.

'So I hailed a taxi outside the motel and just said British Committee and he knew immediately where it was and drove me straight there.'

'And there I was waiting for you, in such a state ever since Kukrit came back late from the airport and said he'd missed you,' Jeremy replies, suggesting with automatic but irrelevant chivalry that they are lovers separated from their tryst with one another.

And here I am, Kate thinks, sitting opposite you and thinking there's more distance between us in terms of class and sex awareness than a million years of chat over drinks at six dollars a go on the Oriental Hotel terrace could ever hope to bridge. She sees herself, a young woman with white limbs and a neat haircut, sitting in a short linen dress, toying with a tall glass of frosted beer, while opposite her lounges an attentive and deferential male. Talking over a drink; the most natural of interactions. Thousands of people do it every day; what's wrong with me that my inside's screaming that it's not real? Cool capable Kate the British Committee librarian confronts Kate the embryonic hysteric, catches her eye for a moment and grimaces with a bitter self-directed humour. If Annie or Jean could see you now, says one Kate to the other, they wouldn't know you. Self-preservation, replies Kate the British Committee librarian feebly, I can't afford a breakdown, this is me for the moment, there's nothing I can do about it.

Jeremy's voice summons her uncomfortably to a mesh of past and present.

'Kidnapped, and by a Thai man at that. . . . It must have been terribly upsetting for you,' says Jeremy's mouth, while his eyes say Go on, admit it, didn't you enjoy it, some of it?

'It was,' says Kate firmly. But you'll never know all the reasons why.

Unwilling to confront a self she hates, she switches subjects awkwardly.

'Didn't you say you knew of some Lao restaurants near here? Let's go and eat — I'm starving.' I don't want to feel, let me push down thinking by eating. Food for thoughts, puns the hysterical Kate as they depart.

Outside after their meal they crouch in the small low car, knees touching chins, Jeremy braced for maximum impact on the controls as he carves a jerky aggressive path through the sluggish traffic. They swoop and scream to a halt in a narrow street alive and garish with neon signs over narrow dark doorways.

'You really must see this,' Jeremy explains as he pockets the ignition key, 'it's the heart of the nightlife area.'

Sure: local colour, interesting ethnic mores, I am a cool intelligent person ready to sample the strange, the colourful, the offbeat, appreciate approaches and lifestyles so different to my own.

They pick a path through the crowded gloom inside to a low table in a corner at the far end. A hostess in tight teeshirt and jeans lingers only long enough to assure Kate discreetly with her eyes that she is not poaching on her territory, smiles velvetly at Jeremy, brings them their drinks. A line of girls sits at the bar, ready at the jerk of a head or the flick of a finger to minister to the solitary Somerset Maughams at every table with drinks, smiles and conversation in carefully-broken Americanisms.

'This is my favourite place,' Jeremy shouts to her above the music, 'fantastic girls here, really alive and witty. They have a girl here on Saturdays, Suzy SevenUp, she can smoke seven cigarettes in her cunt at once.'

'Oh for Christ's sake —' Kate begins, 'then I'm not going to stay —' but she is drowned by a particularly raucous burst from the band. A dazzle of green and red spotlights explodes onto the dais in front of them, revealing a bamboo cage containing a girl naked except for tassels and a G-string. An exquisite bored mobile of gyrating flesh, her arms, legs and stomach caress the music and the customers' eyes. Jeremy is leaning forward, his face rapt, his body taut; other men, more sophisticated, sit back, toying absently with their drinks and their girlfriend's knees as they watch.

Kate feels sick. The spectacle is intended for her too as part of the audience, but she cannot become a pair of eyes to view her own humiliation. That body up there is a female body, not a sexless abstract sculpture; if another woman is being stripped, exposed, graded and sold as an object, then she herself is too. All around her men's eyes are avidly forsaking their embarrassed girlfriends for the fantasy they have paid the go-go dancer to concoct of herself; the room contains a crowd of men united in desire and fear of possession of women who are separated from each other by bars.

Kate wrenches at Jeremy's arm and his attention. Courteously he swings back towards her, his sleepwalker's expression cracking into irritation as she whispers furiously, 'I'm going, I'm not going to stay in here —'

Outside, she plunges across the pavement away from the car, but is stopped by Jeremy's grip on her arm.

'What the hell was all that about?' he demands. 'What's wrong with you, for God's sake?'

'What d'you mean, what's wrong? How on earth d'you expect me to sit there watching that woman being forced to humiliate herself like that?'

Taken aback by her anger and foreseeing the likelihood of her leaving him on the strength of it, Jeremy switches tactics to conciliation.

'Oh, come on, don't be so disapproving. She wasn't being humiliated, she was just doing her job. She's got a lovely body, why should you criticise her for showing it off?' Just because yours isn't as good, her mind fills in the blank space. She turns to face him.

'I'm not criticising her — it's all those men in there, paying her to do it.'

He struggles uneasily.

'That's not the point. She's not being forced to do it. You're just being puritanical.'

'Oh, for God's sake —' Kate exclaims, and tries to wrench her arm away. A crowd of amused onlookers, attracted by the sight of two flushed angry whites arguing with each other in the street, has collected. Any moment now they will press forward, take sides, and, worst of all, possibly even scratch the car's polished paintwork.

Realising too that he is about to lose Kate to her anger and the night, Jeremy forces a pleasanter expression to his face.

'Look, Kate, we can't talk here. I'm sorry, I'm not trying to upset you.' He allows himself a carefully selected smile, humorous, equal to equal, and goes on, the ease of his words belied by the hurry of his delivery and the force of his grip on her arm.

'Don't you think you owe me an explanation of all this? It's all a bit sudden, you know. I'd like to talk to you about it, somewhere quieter. Why not come back to my place for coffee? I'd really like to understand, you know —'

The first edge of her anger gone, Kate hesitates, trapped by the apparent sincerity of his voice more than by the real force of his hand. Unsure of whether she does owe him an explanation, of how much of her perspective she can get across in a conversation, and unwilling to let go of the London Kate who has broken through to the surface, she is ashamed of her suspicions of his reasons for asking her back to his place and agrees.

Jeremy's flat is in the same expensive suburb for whites as her own, part of a concrete block overlooking orchidhouse and swimming-pool. Inside, the polished teak floor is strewn with hilltribe rugs, while a couple of antique carved teak cabinets house an extensive collection of Meo silver jewellery and Sukhothai pots, and the walls are hung with more rugs interspersed with modern paintings. Jeremy settles Kate on a rattan sofa with a whisky, flicks on the stereo and then sits down himself at the other end of the sofa, making sure that she notices his careful maintenance of physical space between them.

He fixes her with his eyes, all eager deferential intelligence, while his hands busy themselves rolling a joint.

'What I don't understand is why you didn't say all this before. I had no idea you didn't approve of go-go dancing or I'd never have taken you there.'

She sighs.

'I don't disapprove of go-go dancers. I hate the system that forces them to do it for a living and then screws them afterwards.'

He winces. 'But they're so lovely, they enjoy it. And what's wrong if they do? It's a better way of making a living than digging the roads.'

'Look — first, who are you to decide which women are lovely and which aren't? The whole nightclub scene runs on women trying to approximate to impossible male standards of beauty. And second —'

He passes her the joint. 'Buddha grass,' he murmurs, 'the main reason for staying in this god-awful country —'

She inhales deeply and goes on.

'And second, what makes you think they enjoy it? They're paid to smile, don't you realise that? It just makes you feel good because you kid yourself they'd do it for free anyway.'

She takes a second hit, hauls a bullet of dope down into her lungs and continues.

'And the women who dig the roads have to go home and be screwed by their husbands afterwards as part of the job. The point is that the one exploitation is part of the other, either way women are treated as shit.'

Kate passes the joint back to Jeremy. He inhales deeply, blows a series of perfectly matched smokerings at the ceiling. Could Suzy SevenUp blow them as well?

'OK, fine, I take your point. But why didn't you tell me before that you believed in women's lib? Sorry —' Catching sight of her irritated expression. 'That you were a feminist? You walk around in a skirt and wear a bra, how was I to know?'

'Look, I came out here in a muddle. I already hate myself for having taken the job, I know it was a mistake. I can't even criticise the setup objectively, I just know that I'm unhappy. Because I've compromised so much on who I thought I was. But can't you see how you're defined by the situation you're in? If I didn't wear a skirt none of the Thais I work with in the library would respect me. They'd freak totally, if their boss went around in jeans. And because I feel unhappy and insecure here I cover up on what I really think because I'm scared to let it out and confront people.'

She stops, surprised at her willingness to expose herself to him. Her only friend, is that it? Like Sadat on another occasion? Jeremy murmurs sympathetically and hands her back the joint. She takes a deep drag and goes on.

'And fuck it, it's not just about the clothes that people wear. I mean, I don't see how I can be involved here politically, it's not my place. I've just got a set of opinions, that's all, to hand out when the occasion arises. Dinner table radical chick, that's all I am.'

She stops, before her bitterness turns into more self-hatred. The room lurches. She goes on slowly and naively: 'I'm really glad, in a way, that you took me to that place. It really pushed things out. Yet —'

Her mouth goes soft and woolly, expands rapidly to become a cave; her tongue is a red seal lolling there, a sea anemone blurring in a flower of shadow. She is a body in a room; she is the room; her head takes off to become a camera snapping and exposing the million thoughts flashing through her brain every second. She booms and whispers, shrinks and expands. She gropes with her hands in the air. Two arms seize her, Jeremy's voice shouts to her and whispers, 'It's OK, keep cool, I'm here.'

He is stroking her back, kissing her face. She struggles, irritated that he hasn't realised what she'd wanted. He pushes her on to the floor and lies on top of her, nearly smothering her.

'Don't,' she manages feebly to say from wherever she is, 'I'm all right, leave me alone.'

Her fault, obviously, to have felt for his hand. His hands and his body are everywhere, suffocating her. She is so slowed down by the dope slamming fifty visions of hell at her a second that she finds it hard to fight, hard to believe in her own anger, hard to believe in what she's doing. So why bother to struggle? This can't be happening to me, Kate would never get herself into this sort of situation.

They roll clumsily on the floor for about half an hour, his tongue making constant assaults on her mouth until her face is wet with saliva and tears, her neck aches from turning her head from side to side to avoid his mouth and her jaw from clamping itself shut. She is a stiff bundle of rags, arching this way and that, legs clamped together against his knees' efforts to prise them apart, arms straining him back up off her body. Eventually she manages to deliver a particularly nasty jab and he gives up. They roll apart and she looks at him with sullen exhaustion, her head still pumping in and out. He gazes at her with puzzled concern.

'Look, it had to come some time, you know. There's always that barrier to be got over, when you are going to sleep with someone for the first time, and I just thought it would be a good time to get it over with. Don't get so upset, it's part of every relationship.'

'With a woman,' she mutters through bruised lips.

He sighs. 'I'm sorry, Kate, I really am. I had no idea you'd react that way. You took my hand, after all.'

She slumps back on the floor, still finding it nearly impossible to speak as every word that emerges takes on new lives and dimensions of its own. Only her anger gives her the energy to lift her arm to look at her watch. 3 a.m.

'You'd better sleep here,' Jeremy replies cheerfully to her unspoken statement. 'I'm too tired to run you home and you won't get a taxi at this time of night. You'll have to share my bed though, there's nowhere else.'

He jumps to his feet, smooths back his hair, goes briskly into the bedroom, crashes around in the bathroom. She stumbles after him, and lies down on the bed. As soon as she closes her eyes, the kaleidoscope takes over again.

Lek, the thirty-year-old maid installed for her along with the furniture by the Committee, telling her about the nine children and the mother up-country she supports and whom she rarely sees. Lek sleeps in a concrete cell downstairs where husbands are forbidden by the landlord to visit. Lek's husband has taken another woman. The other maids in the block all angry when guilty Kate gives Lek a rise. The woman official from USAID living in the flat above purring over Campari about the servant problem. The British ladies withdrawing, after their dinner from the frozen stores of English food flown into the Embassy shop, to powder their noses before flowing eagerly back to their men sipping brandy on the terrace under trees prodigal with flame-of-the-forest blossoms. The heavy makeup melting even in the air-conditioning, the legless beggar who sleeps under the office porch and cleans their shoes in gratitude, the slums you cannot observe because no roads go through the swamps and whose inhabitants do not exist for the State because the census officials cannot reach them, the bomb-carriers serving as flower-pots, the boys selling themselves to the rich English ex-public schoolboys, the girls selling themselves to the fat German tourists, the police raping the boys and the girls they are protecting in the police-stations, the Committee officers boasting to Kate about the elegant jerk-offs in the massage parlours, their ever-decorative ever-bored wives boasting to Kate about their jewellery, the Thai girls saving up for eye and breast jobs, the luxury hotels where the high-class white whores hang out, the students shot by the military during a demonstration against the army regime, the girl students daring for the first time to stay out at night on the streets to picket, the crushing of strikes with bullets and beatings, the barring of political books in the Committee library, the anti-Communist adverts punctuating the Western films on TV. The office drivers buying her fierce Singha beer and teaching her to dance the Ramwong, and her library assistants taking her to markets and on river trips, bringing her sticky cakes and jasmine garlands and inviting her to their homes. The scent of jasmine in her flat at night, shouting her loneliness.

The Committee Representative will describe Kate's anger as culture shock, in his report on her work to HQ. She's very young, only a girl really, and it takes time to get used to this funny little country.

Jeremy switches off the light, lies down beside her. At his exploring touch she jerks upright.

'Fuck off, we've been through all that. Just leave me alone, OK?'

'You're unreasonable,' he snarls, and turns away from her. She lies with her eyes open, listening to his noisy jerking-off and then his snores.

He drives her to work next day, humming unconcernedly into her silence.

She sits in the Representative's office, smoking too many cigarettes. He has placed them both on the sofa under the magnificent painting of a Ramayana demon by his Thai protegé, not facing one another across his huge desk, to indicate that this is an intimate and informal interview, not to be taken too seriously whatever she says.

Laugh, Kate, and I'll take you out to supper at this amusing little noodle shop I've discovered in Chinatown. Be a pal, Kate, and slip me the copy of Gay News you hide under your desk because I don't allow it in the library, talk about work, Kate, discuss how we spend £5000 on economics books for the university libraries, tell me about how you're stopping the students thieving my favourite art books, but please for God's sake, Kate, don't be difficult, don't talk about imperialism and marxism and feminism, I've heard it all before and said it all myself, twenty years ago before I had a wife and children to support.

She yields to his pressure and obscures her political statements by bursting into tears. Relieved, Andrew pats her shoulder.

'Never mind,' he says kindly, 'the heat gets on top of all of us, you know. Why not take a couple of days off work? The library staff can manage on their own for a little while, I'm sure.'

Although his head and body are bent towards her in paternal concern, their tension indicates that he wants to be elsewhere; away from hysterical females, generally, and, in particular, at his lunchdate with the Chinese antique dealer who has hinted over the telephone that he has some particularly fine pieces of Ban Chieng that the National Museum will never see hidden away in his back room.

Humiliated, Kate blows her nose ungracefully and almost apologises for not knowing what has come over her.

'I'm leaving,' she says firmly, 'I want to hand in my notice.'

With amazement and with pleasure she hears her own voice saying No.

Acts of Violence
Zöe Fairbairns

Although it was Dorothy who had come to interview the officials at PopCon ('an Intergovernmental Agency for Fundamental Research into the Worldwide Problems of Population Stabilisation'), she kept getting the impression that it was they who were interrogating her.

'What are you after?'

'Who do you work for — really?'

'Whose side are you on?'

'Aren't you grateful for the money?'

Dorothy explained that they hadn't given *her* any money; she was here as a reporter for a journal whose name they knew; her membership of the feminist abortion campaign to which PopCon had just made a large grant was irrelevant to the present discussion; she was just doing her job.

'Yeh, doing your job, seeing weird and wonderful conspiracies everywhere,' said the clipped-haired, clipped-voiced man behind the desk, the Press Liaison Officer. 'Your group better watch out. If they don't want the money —'

Dorothy scoffed. 'You know quite well you can't take it back. I just wonder why you gave it in the first place.'

'And you're suggesting —'

'No, I'm *asking*. Now, are you prepared to let me look at your research programme or not?'

'Not if you're going to use it for lies, propaganda and distortion,' said the Press Liaison Officer.

She got up, grinning. 'I'll be off, then.'

'We don't want to be obstructive, Miss Lenham, we want to help the press all we can, and there's nothing secret in what we do here, nothing whatever. But if we give you information, how do we know you won't distort it?'

'You don't,' she said, sitting down. 'But if you won't let me see unsecret information, I can distort *that* too.'

The Press Liaison Officer took a heavy file from a shelf and almost dropped it into her hands; but she had strong wrists and managed a gracious smile of acceptance and thanks.

'My colleagues and I will be very interested,' he said sourly, 'to know what kind of propaganda that red magazine you work for can make out of an international survey of prospective parents' attitudes to the impending birth.'

'You've got to be kidding!' yelped Margaret Lenham, as much aston-ished as afraid at the sight of what he planned to use for the operation: a knitting needle. A knitting needle, in this day and age! It had been good enough in the bad old days, good enough for her mother before her, good enough, in all probability, for her grandmother too, if the secrets of that angelic white head were ever known. But you expected something better nowadays, especially for a woman in her forties! 'It is . . . clean, isn't it?'

'There's nothing to worry about, Mrs L,' he said, 'I know my work.' And the years rolled away, and it was a different room yet still the same, the room where she'd had her first; old white paint with the grudging cleanliness of not quite enough scrubbing; the sticky rubber mat under her bottom, that made her wonder about all the other bottoms that had lain on it, wonder desperately to take her mind off the panic at the instrument's entry into her, and the thought, *it's like the first screw you ever had — why do we do it, why do we go on doing it?*

'No,' she said. 'No.' She felt the cold steel hesitate.

'I haven't hurt you?'

'I don't want to.'

'Of course you do.'

'No, I'm — we — we women, we're impulsive in middle age, you know. Change our minds a lot.'

'You'll have to let me finish now that I've started,' he said.

She raised her head and looked at him between her bare knees. He looked quizzical, concerned — almost personal about her. *Who the hell did he think he was?*

'Get-out-of-me!' Her body heaved, and his hurtled across the room under the unexpected blow from her foot. She fled home on the underground, scolding herself for being such a coward, it could be all over now if she'd been sensible. Or if she'd known where to go to get it done properly. She could have asked Dorothy of course, Dorothy knew about these things, but she couldn't face the look of exasperation she knew she'd get, the telling-off. She ran bleak eyes along the row of advertisements: bad breath, jobs for temps, are you pregnant? 'Yes!' she said in surprise. 'How clever of you — it doesn't show yet, surely?' People sitting next to her got up and moved away. She read the advertisement carefully: they helped you if you were pregnant! Well, she was going to need a lot of help, that was for sure, and if someone took the trouble to put an advert in the tube, the least you could do was memorise the number. The things she was going to need for the baby! She started to make a list in her head.

Dorothy, Margaret's daughter, looked round the two-room flat that was their home, and groaned. So it had been a collection day today. Mother had been making collections. Eighteen milk bottles on the mantelpiece, some with milky smears and doubtless smelling cheesy. Rusty tins under the bed and a few more in the sink. And in a carrier bag, cunningly at the back of a cupboard, a bumper harvest of old newspapers.

Mother must have something on her mind.

'Oh *mother* —' She heard tears in her voice. She was tired.

'It's all right, dear, I'm going to wash everything, and either keep it or sell it.'

'Keep old baked bean tins?' Dorothy fought the anger that was so debilitating, so futile. 'Sell dirty newspapers?' Mother couldn't help it. Things could be worse.

'The other way round, dear. Tins can be recycled. Perhaps the newspapers weren't such a good idea. Not very hygienic for —'

'OK, mother, but please clear it, and will you get dinner tonight, I have to write something very urgently —'

Closing her mind to her mother was a survival skill Dorothy had learned many years ago when she realised that if she didn't look after her, no-one else was going to. Then it became the only way to work: shut mother out, shut out her demands, her outrages, concentrate, work. It might seem brutal sometimes, but there was no point in having two people mad.

'. . . don't you think, dear?'

'Mother, I'm not discussing anything now. I'm working.' She got out her PopCon notes, started arranging things in her mind. Start with a punchy sentence, get them reading. Then the facts, the evidence. Then the guesses, the speculations, the comments, the careful qualifications, the neat manipulation of emphasis. But which was which? Was it true? Was any of it true? Did her excitement at the way the evidence fitted together mean she wanted it to be true? And if it was true, was any purpose served by revealing it — any purpose other than the advancement of her own career?

'Dorothy, how would you feel about it if I —'

'Mother, I can't support us if I can't work.'

Margaret fell silent. Dorothy was relieved. Something had apparently been decided, for Margaret's continuous muttering stopped and she went silently about the business of washing the tins. At least she only robbed bins and doorsteps, she didn't shoplift. If she screwed around, at least she was discreet. She was continent and clean and was usually OK to go out by herself. And she wasn't violent. She wasn't really violent like other mad people.

A few days later, one of the cheaper newspapers headed a story: 'SCIENCE CONFIRMS: TOO MANY WOMEN!' The text said:

'Science has finally confirmed what many a mere male has long suspected — that the troubles of the world are women's fault, and if there were fewer of them, things would get on a whole lot better.

This news was given to the world last night, at, of all things — a women's lib meeting!

Posing as a libber, one of our reporters attended a secret meeting of a pro-abortion group and heard its leader, journalist Miss Dorothy Lenham, warn the "sisters" that the funding given to the campaign by the presitigious international research foundation PopCon, might well have sinister implications.

"PopCon has been doing research all over the world to establish that the majority of prospective parents would prefer a son to a daughter, and many would be prepared to undergo minor medical procedures to ensure that they got their wish, including the abortion of a female fetus," Dorothy told a hushed audience in a room at a secret address in North London. "PopCon regards this as the final solution to the population problem, since a predominantly male population will obviously produce fewer babies than one in which the sexes are evenly matched.

"They are investing in the development of a pill that will ensure male-only births. But in the meantime, some of their researchers think it sufficient to promote sex-tests for unborn babies together with abortion on demand."

Challenged after the meeting by our reporter and asked if she was not being a bit melodramatic, Dorothy said: "It is disgraceful that you have gatecrashed a private meeting like this, and reported on thoughts that have not been fully developed yet. Wait until I've written a full report."

But did Dorothy not agree that cutting down on women might be a solution to the population problem in the third world? "Birth control isn't just about the population problem, it's about women's autonomy," she said. "We aren't breeding machines, to be phased out when no more breeding is required."

Cartoon, page 7.'

Dorothy woke, tense and listening. There was someone in the corridor.

She held her breath. The lighted dial of her watch said one-twenty. Mother was drawing great rambling breaths and muttering. There was no stir in the flat. The footsteps passed on — someone for the people upstairs. Her conscience had woken her, not the footsteps. She'd hardly spoken to mother all day. She'd tried to keep the newspaper story hidden from her because she didn't want to discuss it until she'd had more time to get her thoughts in order . . . but of course mother had found it and started questioning compulsively about abortion, what exactly was the law on it now, how did you get one, where did you go, what did it cost, things she must have heard Dorothy and her friends discussing a hundred times but which the newspaper report had triggered into today's obsession.

Damn, damn, damn that bloody newspaper, why couldn't they give people five minutes to discuss something important without destroying everything with their hysteria and filthy ridicule?

How was a person supposed to think straight when —?

A world without women! No — not quite without. Some would be needed, there would have to be some breeding. Others would be borne by the few feminists and freaks who preferred girls, for the whole thing would be voluntary; no compulsion would be needed; PopCon's research had been thorough. In a few generations, of course, people would want girls again, and values and fashions would change . . . but in the meantime, what would it be like to be one of an endangered species?

What would the world be like? A universal rotary club, or army barracks, or Dartmoor prison, or Ku Klux Klan, or Catholic priesthood or boardroom or Eton or Glasgow gang! There was no lack of models.

The doorbell rang. Dorothy fled to it. Through the letter box she hissed: 'Sssh, shh, please, my mother's very —'

'Dorothy. We have to talk to you.'

'Who is it?'

'You don't know us.'

She opened the front door and stepped out into the corridor, which was more private than the flat if mother was only pretending to be asleep, which was possible.

She faced two women, one short and tough-looking in a military jacket; the other pale, blonde, anaemic, with watery eyes.

'We read about you in the papers,' said the anaemic one.

'Who are you, though?'

'I'm Lula, this is Claire.'

'I can't ask you in. My mother —'

'We have to talk somewhere,' said Claire, the tough one, who was rather frightening.

'We could go for a walk,' said Dorothy.

She dressed while they waited, then they went down the greasy stairs into the street. The two strangers flanked Dorothy, making her wonder, as she had at the PopCon building, whether she could get away. Not that she wanted to; the cold silence of the night was itself a release from the warm clammy room and her mother's muttered claims on her, claims from which there would be no escape until death. Three pairs of footsteps clattered on the pavement, out of step, like three clocks. Lula and Claire were talking to her, a sort of duet: Lula was persuasive and chatty, Claire chimed in with sharp ideological comments or scornful snorts: hard cop, soft cop.

'I don't know,' said Dorothy softly when they wanted an answer from her. 'I don't know at all.'

'How can you *not know*?'

'We understand the difficulty,' said Lula gently. 'But we — Claire, and I, and a lot of other women — have been wondering how much longer you were going to make money writing articles about the women's movement before you felt a duty to take some kind of action.'

'I didn't write that article —'

'No, they got in first, but you were planning to. You must make quite a lot of money —'

'I make my living and I support my mother!' Dorothy looked wildly around her as if for an escape — but nothing was restraining her. 'I might get my arms blown off, I need them for my work! Who are you, anyway?'

'We're a group of women who are tired of talk.'

'What would it achieve — supposing I did it? Why me?'

'Why you, because you know the building and could get into it. A follow-up story or something. As to what it would achieve . . .' Claire abandoned the explanation, Lula took her cue.

'It's symbolic. Every woman who read about what that place is for will understand. It's an act of solidarity with every woman who's under pressure to have a baby, or have a boy or have a girl or who knows, for god's sake, have a puppy or a kitten or a goddamned foal.'

'I know.' Dorothy bit her nails miserably. 'I know. But what are we saying? All those bastards want is to let people choose the sex of their baby. What can we say against that?'

'You talk as if it was an interesting academic problem,' Claire snarled. 'Don't you realise they want to *wipe us out*? Can we really do nothing about it, just because they seem to have taken one of our slogans, one of our demands and twisted it? Why did you go after the story in the first place if your position wasn't clear?'

Dorothy said, 'I have to live.'

'So do we all, sister.'

'What would I have to do . . . if I agreed.'

'Just go in there and leave a package.'

'Is that all?'

'That's all.'

'OK.'

Margaret heard Dorothy go out. Something connected with her work presumably . . . poor Dorothy, working all hours! Dorothy thought her efforts weren't appreciated, but oh, they were, they were. Margaret knew she wasn't the easiest person to live with, she knew she had her mad days, but Dorothy tolerated, accepted, got on with her career.

Margaret couldn't inflict a baby on her.

'Doctor, I'm pregnant.'

The doctor grinned. 'At your age?' He looked young enough to be her son. 'You should give it up, you know,' he said. 'It's bad for the heart.' He scribbled on a pad. 'Still, a short life but a merry one, eh? Take that along to the hospital.'

She got up and went to the door. She'd been in the surgery exactly two minutes. He looked up. 'It was an abortion you wanted, wasn't it?'

'Yes, doctor. Thank you very much doctor.'

When she got to the hospital, they gave her an appointment to see a gynaecologist in six weeks time.

So she went instead to the place that advertised on the tube that it helped you if you were pregnant; she thought there might be the small chance that they would know where she could get an abortion. Desperation was beginning to seize at her guts; Dorothy had tolerated so much from her, but she would not take this. *Mother, I can't support us if I can't work*, she always used to say when she wanted a bit of peace and quiet . . . what chance of peace and quiet with a baby in the tiny flat? Dorothy would leave and abandon her at the very idea. She wasn't going to tell that fear to anyone though; she wasn't having them prying or saying that Dorothy ought to be glad of a new brother or sister.

She rang the number she'd seen on the underground and went to the address they told her.

'If you promise not to tell anyone,' Margaret said, when she finally got to see a doctor, 'I nearly had it done the old way, you know, with a knitting needle, then I lost my nerve.'

She thought telling him that would prove she was determined.

'Would you like to tell me why you want an abortion?'

'I just do, that's all.'

'Yes, but why?'

'Why do I have to tell *you*?'

'I'm the one who you're asking to do it,' said the doctor, reasonably. He leaned forward. 'Look, it's up to you. As far as *I'm* concerned, it's on demand. But I have to have something to go on your notes, see? Just in case we're ever investigated.'

So Margaret started to tell him. Afterwards she couldn't remember half of what she'd said. If she'd meant to lie, she'd have planned the lies; as it was, it was more like someone else speaking, someone for whom all the tales might be true: the tales of the amorous husband who would not be denied, or even delayed; of her horrified discovery that her tried and trusted dutch cap had let her down after all these years, of her disappointment that she would not now be able to train as a doctor or run a campaign for more zebra crossings or offer a home to her poor ailing mother; and then of course there were the medical difficulties, what with her diabetes and the early mongol child that died and all those Caesarians; and the home where there wasn't an inch of space and how the baby would mean eviction and bankruptcy; and the fear that the baby might be too obviously of mixed-race; and the over-riding, gut-rending terror that the baby might have royal blood (of course if ever this got outside these walls there would be no answering for the political consequences for the western world) and in the circumstances it seemed kind that the child should never be born.

'Come in the day after tomorrow,' he said. 'You'll only have to stay one night.'

He couldn't have believed all that, surely?

If she was going to be in the hospital for one night she would need lots of things to read. Or maybe they supplied them. They hadn't told her that and she would need to know. If she had to take her own reading things she ought to start collecting them now, whereas if they supplied them it would be embarrassing to turn up with a bag of newspapers, as if you didn't know how to behave. She would have to phone them. It was a stupid thing to phone to ask but she would have to. She realised in a panic that she had forgotten the number. Well — kill two birds with one stone. Down into the Central Line, pick up abandoned newspapers and look for that advertisement. She found it quite easily. It was a funny advertisement, it didn't come right out and say it gave you abortions, it just promised to 'help'. Why not come out and say it in this day and age, she muttered to herself as she dialled the number.

'Hello, this is Mrs Lenham, look about my abortion the day after tomorrow, I just wanted to know if . . .'

'You're having an abortion?'

'Sorry, I mean I'm pregnant and, er, you said you could help me the day after tomorrow and I wanted to know if . . .'

'We can help you *today*, Mrs Lenham.'

'What —?'

'The positive way.'

The woman's voice made her realise something was wrong.

'You're not the place I —'

'You may have got the wrong number, dear, but it's a stroke of luck for you . . . and for your baby.'

'It's not a baby, it's a lump of jelly!'

Margaret panicked, she'd got the wrong number, the wrong place, the wrong advertisement, why didn't they get off the line, why didn't they leave her —

'It's a baby. It has arms and legs. If you were to touch him with a pin — and he's a boy or a girl by now — he'd move away, he feels pain. If you cut him up and pulled him out of your body — which is what they do —'

'Oh you liar, you liar, you're lying you liar!' She banged down the phone, rushed from the station. How dare anyone tell her what to do? She'd choose, she'd decide, it was her body, her life.

The fire at the PopCon building was big news for a day or so. One office was burned out completely, and with it some fairly important papers that would take several months' research to restore. Seven fire engines were called, and traffic was held up all over London. The firm which had fire-proofed the building got high praise for the containment of the blaze. It was clearly a case of arson, but the motive was puzzling at first. The culprit was assumed to be the young woman whose charred body had been trapped by the flames; she was identified as a feminist — funny, when PopCon had been giving money and moral support to feminist groups.

Then the paper that had published the earlier report recognised her name as that of the rather hysterical women's libber who was planning to expose PopCon as the enemy of women . . . and this seemed to clear the matter up. Obviously a one-man operation by a disturbed girl who believed in her own propaganda.

'The cause of female freedom,' warned the paper, 'which we have always supported, is ill-served by terrorism of this kind.'

Margaret called the new baby Dorothy Two.

With Dorothy One so suddenly dead, the abortion had been impossible.

Dorothy Two was a difficult baby. Margaret had to be anaesthetised for the birth, and she was hardly well when they sent the two of them home. Dorothy Two cried all day and cried all night, and Margaret's only respite was when she went to work, to the factory-cleaning job she had had to take. She wished Dorothy One was still there to help, but she was determined to manage. If she didn't manage they'd take the baby away, and then everything would be wasted.

She used to slip home from the factory during her lunch breaks to make sure Dorothy Two was all right. And there she'd be, always crying.

And one day a lady came from the clinic. She was a fat, plain woman in blue overalls, with moles on her face and no wedding ring.

'Good afternoon, Mrs Lenham. We're a bit concerned about Dorothy, we haven't seen you and her for such a long time.'

'She's all right.'

'May I —'

'She's *asleep*!'

Dorothy Two wailed treacherously.

The clinic woman hoisted her into the air and looked at her in distaste. Margaret gasped at the way the child suddenly became thin and feverish-looking under the woman's gaze.

'Have you got a clean towel?'

'What for?' demanded Margaret. 'Whose baby is it, anyway? Whose room? Whose towel?'

'I want to lie her down and have a look at her. Did you *plan* to have this child, dear?'

'I'll put some newspaper on the bed.'

'But that's *dirty* newspaper! Really, this place is very squalid, Mrs Lenham, if you don't mind my saying so.'

'Well, you see, I was going to have an abortion, only —'

'So why didn't you?'

The clinic woman laid her own coat on the bed and put Dorothy Two on it. She poked a finger at the big red raw patches on her thighs.

'Urine burns,' she pronounced; and soon Dorothy Two was taken off into care.

Into care — yes, that was what they called it, care. But who cared? It made her howl with bitterness when she was alone in the weeks that followed, and it made her grit her teeth as she strode through the streets looking for revenge, or for her baby, or for Dorothy, not too sure what she was looking for but usually coming home with nothing better than a bag of old tins.

She phoned a lot of numbers — for London seemed suddenly full of numbers to phone if you wanted help. As well as the numbers to phone if you wanted an abortion or if you didn't, there were numbers for if you felt like committing suicide, were going bald, wanted a job, had been arrested or wanted today's recipe. Margaret tried them all, but none of them had any help for her.

Because there was no help for her. In between bouts of crying and phoning, she knew that. She was bereaved of two daughters. She wished neither of them had ever been born. 'I should have had abortions both times,' she muttered.

But you couldn't really say that. Dorothy One had died for something she believed in (though Margaret was not quite sure what it was), but she'd have helped keep Dorothy Two if she'd lived.

TWO

Feminist fiction and politics

We tell these stories in various camps. We are answered with the questions: 'But what does your feminism have to do with our revolution?' 'What does your socialism have to do with our women's liberation?' 'What does fiction have to do with politics?' We are sisters, colleagues and comrades to each other. I read this book as a declaration of that coalition.

Although I cannot state priorities, I can explain how feminism, socialism and fiction are complementary. I begin by asking other questions, 'How can you be a socialist and *not* be a feminist?' Certainly we will have no revolutionary social change without the insights and vitality of women. This proclamation was made vociferously by the thousands of females who deserted the ranks of the macho Left in the late 1960s. During the last decade, Western women have engaged in anger, introspection, pride, strength, but not yet liberation. We have learned how the exploitation of sexuality, race and class are parallel, integrated mechanisms of capitalism. Liberation means working together toward a coexistence of equals. So, 'How can you have women's liberation *outside* socialism?' We do not want to initiate more lady stockbrokers or big white mamma imperialists. We want to match strength for strength in a larger movement. Which brings the third question, 'How else can we work except with our fiction?' Writing stories is activism. That may sound like an abrupt declamation to you, but it is something we have discussed and argued for eighteen months. We think our politics comes as much from our writers' instincts as our writing is shaped by our politics. Art and activism are not contradictory, but mutually inclusive. You can ask us to write with conscience and skill, but you can't ask us *not* to write.

The political nature of Western art is usually ignored, indeed denied, by critics. The commercial control of the television and record industry indicates the extent popular art is bound up with capitalist interest. From Walt Disney to Nashville (with not a few subtleties in between), the romance about individual opportunity within the present system is a profitable pervasion. Political art takes a less visible, but more explicit, form in Left traditions. Theatre is perhaps the most broadly developed radical medium, including single playwrights like Ibsen and O'Casey; the collective productions of Joan Littlewood's Theatre Workshop; Brecht's Epic Theatre with didactic soliloquies and songs. Although many of us may not have been conscious of it, we were taught political art in school — *A Modest Proposal, War and Peace, The Ragged Trousered Philanthropist* — albeit in safe literary and historical contexts.

Our feminist fiction collective is not original, then, in this connection of art and politics. We hope that we won't be incidental. Each of the stories was written from an assumed or explicit feminist perspective. They go beyond parables about sexism to consider seriously motherhood, lesbianism, marriage, religion, abortion. They are about the Women's Movement as used by middle class institutions and revolutionary organisations, about women as neo-colonialists and as seamstresses. These are all stories we have lived in or written about outside fiction. We think fiction opens a new light, making the stories more personally and politically accessible.

'Women's Fiction' can be salvaged before it stifles in its own mediocrity complex. It has become a hack field, disparaged by writers and feminists. 'Women's' magazines and novels have numbed their readers with mundane, sentimental femininity. These stories attempt to reclaim femininity, to discover, describe and incite women. I don't deny our debt to Jane Austen, George Eliot or Virginia Woolf: our freedom to keep our writing on top of the blotter, in our names, our sanity maintained, indeed proclaimed by our sisters. Nor do I presume to be part of any tradition. I hope men will enjoy our work, but that is not necessary for our validation. These stories suggest that the personal is political, that fiction extends from therapy to propaganda. We think feminist fiction draws subject, theme and language from an imaginative collectivity of readers and writers.

This second section of the book is openly *about* the Women's Movement. We are using our feminist experiences to say to those on the outside, that the Movement is part of our daily lives and to those on the inside, that we have these tender and critical responses. As feminists, we have to get past that simple, satisfying stage where we read all women as victims or heroines, to the next chapter where we acknowledge that sisterhood is variable.

The subjects of these stories — young, schooled, middle class, white — are as familiar as our mirrors. They are variations on one theme: the Women's Movement as a spiritual-psychological-sexual-ideological catharsis. *Parallel Lines* describes the different directions from which women are politicized into the Movement. *Keep it Clean* describes the different directions into which politics may split the Movement. This story is the most polemical and the most exploratory, treating the wages for housework dispute in detailed historical context. Document or fiction? Feminism or politics? You tell us.

I cannot say *what* these stories mean without saying *how* they are written. They are all done visibly and consciously from within the Movement. The collective was important as an influence on the stories' content and as a workstyle, reminding us that writing is not a virtuoso performance. We have discussed aesthetics and language and argued the consciousness of our protagonists. (Is *Rosemary Patan*'s protest just bourgeois individualism? What is beyond the bucolic intimations of *Martha and Mary*? Has Annie betrayed her lover in *After the Ball*?) I am now confident that writing is a job best done in cooperation with other writers. Collectivity is an expressly political statement for storytellers because our work is often venerated as solitary genesis. In presuming to write about our sisters now, we risk your saying you've heard it all before or that none of it will ever happen. But do say something. Write to us with your criticisms or comments. This suggestion is made explicit because people are too often intimidated by print, considering the ideas in books more real or inviolable than their own. Already, I have valued the responses from the five stories which appeared in *Spare Rib*. If a story moves you to discussion or action the circle of collectivity will be complete.

The book is no more — and we hope no less — of a feminist contribution than those of teachers, trade unionists, abortion counsellors, mothers. And this is the moral of the essay: these stories are part of our work within the Women's Movement.

Valerie Miner

After the Ball was Over
Sara Maitland

I met Kelly yesterday. She was eight months pregnant. Despite everything it was one hell of a shock.

I didn't notice at first; I saw her walking down the street in front of me,
and without any hesitation I knew who it was — I hadn't seen her for over
a year, she had cut her hair off short and was wearing a dress, but I knew.

'Kelly,' I shouted and she turned round and shrieked, 'Annie,
darling', and we tried to fall into each other's arms. She managed this
better than I did, presumably having had practice and certainly having
the advantage of knowing in advance that she stuck out about eighteen
inches in front of where she ought to have been. As I said, it was a shock
and I was clumsy. She didn't seem to notice. 'O, my dear,' she said, 'how
lovely.' But it was she who was lovely, damn her.

So we entered a genteel teashoppe/cafe which happened to be handy and
ordered coffee, as so often before. It came, repulsive, in genteel cups.

'I'm married,' she said, not quite without agression, but not bad.

'So I heard. You didn't ask me to the wedding.' We both grinned
experimentally.

'You wouldn't have liked it, my great-aunt was there.'

'Is he nice?' I asked, I had to say something.

'Absolutely,' she said and glowed. I couldn't help remembering: the
second time we met she had asked the party at large, 'Are there any twin
comets?' 'What?' 'Twin comets?' she'd repeated. 'Because that's what
Annie and I are going to be. We will lighten up the dreary Brighton sky
and dim the fluorescent pier.' She was drunk, but it was not a prophesy
or even a sexual invitation, it was an expression of delight. And now she
was saying with the same delight, about someone else, 'Absolutely.'
Then after a long pause she added, 'Absolutely nice. But do I love him?
Yes. But why? Ah, there's the rub. ''The urge to beget is blind and
sinister.'' It is also confusing.'

'What's that from?' I pounced on the quotation because she had no right, no right at all to burden me with her doubts, after a year, and after everything.

'Translation by Auden of poem by unpronounceable Czech. Also true.' But she knew at once why I had asked and went on with hardly a break for punctuation, 'Well, love, what's with you? I heard you were living with a cabinet member's daughter and fighting for Gay Rights in East Cheam?' We laughed, more easily this time.

'Putney. And her Dad is not a Cabinet Minister. An MP, bourgeois Labour, you know, votes for Comprehensives and sends his kids to public school. Votes for anti-discrimination and throws Lucy out of the house for fear of moral contamination. Poor Lucy, he's a dreadful embarrassment to her, nearly as bad as she is to him.' Kelly laughed again, but for one moment I was afraid she'd do something awful like ask if Lucy was pretty, or something. Quickly I said, 'And where have you been? Making Quiche Lorraine in the suburbs, or bacon and egg pie in some more working class district?'

'Don't be such a goddam bitch,' but she said it affectionately. Then she looked at me almost slyly. 'Actually I saw you at the Central Conference last month.' Then with more confidence, 'And at the abortion thing in May.'

That did surprise me, and hurt. 'Why the fuck didn't you make your presence known?'

'Look at me. I'm pregnant. I didn't feel up to the snubs your radical feminist friends would have handed out.'

'They are NOT radical feminists.'

'Well they bloody looked like it.'

'You're one to talk. Who wouldn't join a Marxist reading group because he was an antiquated masculist, who couldn't recognise the glory of women in struggle?'

'Did I really say that? Ever?'

'Yes, you did. Is that really why you didn't come and chat?'

'Sort of. Unless you're about forty-five and come from Bradford or Stepney and already have about nine children who've brought you to recognise your oppression, there's a big down on pregnancy.'

'Bull.'

'Think about it Annie.' I did.

'All right, not bull. But it's not without reason. A baby. Marriage. Embrace your oppression as masochistically as possible.'

'You're joking. I choose to have a baby like you choose to be gay.'

'I didn't choose to be gay. I am gay.'

'I didn't choose to be womb and boob endowed. I am.'

'Not the same.'

'No, you're right, it's not the same. But it's still my right to choose my own form of sexual self-determination. Anyway, you can see I feel confused about it still, because I couldn't face the flak from your friends. Also of course I didn't know how you'd feel about it.'

'That's nearer the truth.' But we were getting too near the truth. I searched for something different to say and really put my foot in it:

'You've stopped smoking.' And as soon as I'd said it I realised how odd it was, Kelly without a cigarette, without fiddling with the packet and dropping matches on the floor.

'Yes,' she said, 'I had to.'

Just following the flow of words I said, 'Oh. Why?'

She looked away and said, 'Because of the baby.'

Trying to pull us both up short she started on a lecture on the foetal damage caused by nicotine, but neither of us was listening; we were looking at a memory. Kelly sitting hunched in the corner of our vast mattress, with burn holes in our beautiful sheets and an overflowing ashtray beside her, looking into one of the half-dozen cigarette packets and suddenly screaming, 'You fucking bitch, you've finished the goddam bloody cigarettes.' Then after a long while, during which neither of us could escape from her hatred and savagery, she'd said tiredly, 'OK, Annie, we can't do it. Get on the bloody telephone.' And without one word, even of acknowledgement, I had got up and gone downstairs and telephoned.

'Jesus, Kelly, I'm sorry.'

'Don't be. It would never have worked. I've met women since who've done it, and seem to be together all right. I always want to ask them. But it wouldn't have worked for us.'

'Too young?'

'Mm, maybe. But not just that.'

'Come on, Miss Wisdom of the Ages 1977, try and clarify.'

'We never talked it out properly; why I wanted the baby, because it was I, not us, that wanted it, true? Why I wanted it and how that ties in with who I can love, get it together with, I mean long term.'

'Sounds neurotic. Freud calls it masochism.'

'Let him. As of when was he the feminist gospel. Anyway, it's not neurotic, it's a fact of life, a biological, evolutionary thing. At least, a psycho-physiological thing.'

'Get off it, Kelly, you can't posit norms like that.'

'I'm not positing norms. I'm . . . let me see, what am I doing? Clinical case-histories. My own, anyway. It's not, I'm Normal, you're Queer. It's more . . . mm . . . would you buy "bio-chemical predisposition"?'

'No. Nor androgen therapy for gay guys.'

'It's not the same. I'm not trying to cure anything. I'm trying to analyse a quite common fact. That some women want to have children and some don't. I don't see what's so sinister about biology as a hypothesis. Biologically pregnancy clearly suits me. See how great I look.'

'Narcissist,' I said, wanting to get her back into the subject; but she dropped it.

'Yes? No, I don't think . . . not sure. Funny, if we'd been more discreet we'd have got away with it.'

'Relationships belong in the public political sphere.'

'Damn, Annie, stop quoting me at me. I know. That's why you, if anyone, ought to understand why Dick and I got married. Socialise a private relationship. But it is more risky. All our beloved friends.'

'Not just. I couldn't forgive you him.'

'Who?'

'Harry.'

Once we'd decided to have a baby we had had to find a Father. The Father had been Harry. It had been a hellish week. Kelly and he had been so calm and businesslike, and yet . . . I found myself hating them, hating myself for hating them, hating myself for wanting to say so, hating them for putting me in a position of wanting to say so. Insane. I found myself obsessed with voyeuristic sub-passions; I wanted to watch them, I would not say so. One horrible night I found myself crouched at the door, listening for sounds of pain which would have given me pleasure, sounds of pleasure that would have hurt.

'Harry?' exclaimed Kelly. 'Good lord.'

'I was afraid you'd enjoy it too much.'

'Perhaps I did.' After a pause she added, 'I knew you were jealous. There's worse than that. I was glad you were. But we could have worked that through. It was Carol and Bill who shook me.'

Once we knew she was pregnant we'd felt great, and proud. I think we were near deluding ourselves that Harry had never happened, that we'd done it all ourselves. Parthenogenesis, or something, though neither of us was exactly virginal. That week and the waiting afterwards had hurt us, we wanted to be admired, to have our courage and convictions praised, to show off. We'd always been boastful, conspicuous, triumphalist in our love; now we had to tell the World. Which in practice turned out to mean Carol and Bill, these friends of Kelly's. I didn't go with her and I never knew what happened. I came home later and found Kelly shaken.

'What did they say?'

'They gave me the address of a doctor.'

'Great. Who is he? Only the best for my girl.'

'An abortionist.'

'But we don't need a fucking abortionist,' I'd said, 'we want a bloody mid-wife.'

'Thanks,' she'd said, and everything seemed to be all right.

'You're right,' I said now, 'they really laid it on us. Half the people I know came up and condoled with me on your 'Infidelity'. *And* they thought I was being pathetic to put up with it.'

'Well, we'd been so public I suppose everyone thought they had a right to make it their business, and what's more according to us they did.'

The pressures had been heavy and from every direction.

'You must be mad.'

'You two bring up a kid, you have got to be joking.'

'What a sell out.'

'Look, Kelly, if you can't get the money together I'll lend it. Honestly, I'd be more than willing, you poor thing.'

'God, Annie, does she still have it off with blokes, you'd better watch it.'

'Say, Annie, are you both bi, or just Kelly.'

'What does whoever the Father is think?'

'Why tie yourselves down?'

'What's the good of going on about contraception when you can't even get your own head together.'

'You must be mad.'

We started at each other:

You never wanted this baby.

You preferred it with him, didn't you? didn't you? didn't you?

You're jealous, aren't you? aren't you? aren't you?

An agonising visit to this doctor.

'And what makes you think you qualify under the law?'

Kelly had looked at me, I hadn't looked at her. 'I'm a lesbian,' she'd said.

'In that case, no possible problem. Of course. Of course.'

He confirmed what everyone was saying. In fact he confirmed it so strongly that we had pulled ourselves together for a few days.

Locked in each other's arms. We want this baby. We want our baby. We want this baby.

'Ring me up,' the doctor had said, 'when you've made up your mind.' Because he believed that she would make it up, he knew she would, damn him. He never said one single word to me.

'We just weren't brave enough,' I said to Kelly now, 'we thought we were so unconventional and clever and we were wrong. A little more sense and courage, a little less bravado, we'd still be together.'

'No. If we hadn't tried we'd have split up anyway. And I'd have eaten you up with guilt and bitterness first. It was worth a go.'

'I prefer to believe we weren't brave enough. I refuse to submit to being biologically determined in that simplistic way.'

'It's not just biology. It's history and sociology as well. Of course we refuse to be biologically determined in that simple sense; but biology is integrally us. I don't want, no, I refuse to deny my body. Absolutely. Point blank. I don't want any denials, puritan denials; but there have to be choices, you can't have everything.'

'I want everything.'

'Of course. So do I, but we change our definitions of everything to fit our most central desires.'

'Pessimist.'

'Me?'

'Or cynic.'

'Not that.' A pause. Kelly grinned. 'Do you still hate vomit?'

One morning Kelly was sick. Not just a little sick, but very sick indeed. I hate vomit, I can't help it, I simply hate it. I couldn't touch her because she stank of it. I tried but she sensed my revulsion. She sat hunched on the bed all day, silent and smoking. I resented her silence too, it cut me out. All day. I sat and watched her. I couldn't stop myself thinking of the nights she had spent with Harry and wanting to know how much she had enjoyed them. I tried to tell myself I loved her and when that did no good I tried telling myself I hated her. We just sat there not looking at each other, all day, until she burst out with all that anger, 'You fucking bitch you've finished the goddam bloody cigarettes.' It wasn't even true. The anger went out of her eyes, she was exhausted, she surrendered. 'OK, Annie, we can't do it. Get on the bloody telephone.' I was exhausted too. I didn't think of her; I can't say I went because I respected her decision or because I thought it was in her interest; I knew it wasn't in her interest, or mine, or ours. I did it because I was exhausted, and defeated. I rang up the doctor. I was so cowed that I didn't even say who I was; I pretended to be her. The doctor was all compliance. A sensible decision, made in good time. We could do it on the National Health.

For the next few days we made love with a kindliness and consideration we had never experienced before. I even found I could hold her head and pet her while she threw up. We did not discuss it at all. After the operation she came back and there was nothing there. We talked a lot, made love a little, said nothing and never touched each other. One day I came home and she was packing. I didn't even question her. We both cried and kissed each other, and she said, 'I love you, even I love you. Don't forget.' And I said, 'Yes, I know,' and then she went.

'Yes,' I said, looking round for the waitress to give us more coffee, 'I still hate vomit. Also blood, and menstrual cramps and the thought of labour pains and being stitched up and being woken in the night by a shitty damp bundle and having my tits tugged and bitten, and being mauled around by macho chauvinist piglings who call themselves obstetricians. You bet I hate it still.'

Kelly laughed. 'You're denying the complexities of your biology.'

I said, 'And you, my girl, are denying the simplicities of your lusts.'

After we had drunk the coffee, Kelly said, 'Do you notice that I'm still wearing the blue boots you gave me for my birthday?'

'I noticed.'

'Good.'

'Don't flirt with me, Kelly Edwards.'

'I'm sorry. Look, I have to go. Keep in touch. Come to supper, you'll like Dick.'

'Will I?'

'Yes.' She grinned. 'You have a lot in common.'

'I said *don't*.' But I was grinning too.

'You can be my infant's godmother or something.'

'Sure. Give me a ring.'

'God, Annie, I do like you a lot.'

'Too true alas.'

'Not alas at all. There are far too few likeable people around.' She heaved herself to her feet and leaned over to kiss me. There was real delight there. For both of us. I bet when she gets home she's sulky with her husband; I know I will be with Lucy.

Martha and Mary raise Consciousness from the Dead
Michele Roberts

There is a dead nun in the school chapel. She lies in a glass box in front of one of the side altars separating the school chapel from the one the nuns use, both fronting onto the heavily railed-off sanctuary, surrounded by dusty wax flowers and palms and night-lights winking in ruby glass containers. Sister Martha fights the other novices for the job of cleaning the chapel, for then she is able to enter the sanctuary and dust off the tabernacle itself. Only this holy housework enables her to break the chaplain's privilege of closeness to Jesus. The smell of floorpolish mingles with that of incense, Mary Magdalene wiping Christ's arse with her hair.

My mother got married in black.

You've got long hair too, black hair which you push impatiently away from your face with one hand while gesticulating with the other to make a point as you talk. Talking about childhood in the consciousness-raising group last week, telling you stories. Rapunzel, Rapunzel, let down your hair. That's all I've been able to do all afternoon, sit here like bloody Mariana in the moated grange waiting for the telephone to ring. That'll be lovely, I say politely over the telephone, do come round, it'll be nice to see you.

Mummy, can Jane come to tea? Mummy, can I bring Linda home from school? Mummy, can Liz stay the night? Mummy, why can't she?

You're coming over so that we can discuss the demand that the women's movement is making for free contraception and abortion on demand, and the strategy that our local women's group might develop in struggling for that at a local level, how we relate to other women and groups of women in the area, how the abortion issue relates to other ones. How we relate to other women. I've committed myself to writing some notes on it in cooperation with you so that we can take them back to the group next week to discuss with the others.

We could go away for a weekend together, we could; we could wake up next morning and eat croissants and drink coffee from blue china bowls. We could lie propped up against wide pillows edged with lace, the legs of the bed rooted in a froth of cow parsley, convolvulus thrusting through the wrought-iron bedstead, the blue sky and the clouds more solid than the rows of houses underneath. We could pull the quilt up over our bare shoulders, an oasis on a plain of snow where wolves prowl in the bracken and forests are bleak. I could colonise you with gifts, sow a garden, reap a harvest in you, label you with nicknames as my own variety.

You spend a lot of time in your garden, I know, planting, digging. I mostly just look at mine from the window; I've got to know the walnut tree over a whole year now. My bed is under the window; you might be sitting on it in an hour's time. We have owls in our garden; they cried softly last night as I lay in my glass coffin, Snow White waiting for the fairy to wake her into feminism with a kiss.

There is a dead nun in the school chapel. You'd been to convent school as well, you said. That was when I met you for the first time, last week, at the consciousness-raising group that we started at the women's centre a few weeks ago. Last week it was my turn to talk about my past; in order to become conscious of my pain, in order to understand what's happening now and why.

We carry the memory of childhood like a photo in a locket, fierce and possessive for pain or calm; everybody's past is inviolate, separate, sacrosanct, our heads are different countries with no maps or dictionaries, people walk vast deserts of grief or inhabit walled gardens of joy. 'Tell me about your past,' I began to urge other women, and they to urge me. The women sit in circles talking, they are passing telegrams along battle lines, telling each other stories that will not put them to sleep, recognising allies under the disguise of femininity, no longer smuggling ammunition over back garden walls.

Tell me a story, my little brother used to clamour, tell me a story about knights on white chargers and damsels in distress. Tell me a story to keep the bogeys away. I told the group a story, to keep them entertained, to laugh preferably and not to weep, hiding reality from them and myself with metaphor and rhythm, my face without makeup is vulnerable out on the street.

The bathroom and the lavatory were the only places where I could be myself and on my own. My father used to spend hours on the lavatory smoking and reading the paper; when he finally emerged at my mother's disgusted summons, a rich smell of shit and tobacco would sidle out into the corridor. I would lie for hours in my sea grey with the remains of bubble bath. The hot water had prickled pleasantly at the nameless place at the tops of my thighs when I got in; cooler now, it lapped at the dome of my stomach. Two flannels, draped across this, were mermaids, who swam and flopped and basked on islands of flesh. Somewhere, unseen, hardly formed in my imagination, were ships of princes, sailors, of pirates, coming to spy them, fondle them, lead them resistless away.

My dolls were never babies to be fed and bathed and kissed but the protagonists of enormous adventures. They had distinct personalities: princesses forced to disguise themselves as scullery maids or kidnapped into slavery; heroines who dressed up as boys and lived in camps full of men, performing feats of daring beyond description until discovered in bed or in the bath by the hero and proclaimed as beautiful. My imagination faltered at this point; but I lingered over it, returning over and over again to the discovery of my heroine's and my own female body, and the male contemplation of it.

'Run into the garden and play,' my mother constantly urged us. High fences denied the street, traffic, litter, undesirable kids from the council estate up the road. In autumn my father watched for boys who climbed in to steal his apples but was stumped by their shamelessness even when caught red-handed. The youngest son always knew it was only he who would pass the ogre and find the Grail. In winter the bare trees were florid with the purple and grey of pigeons, and in spring we buried dead baby sparrows under the soapsuds of fallen blossom. Between the primary school at the top of the hill and the safe back garden gate the crazy man danced, arms outstretched to catch us, prick flapping between the loose folds of his overcoat.

Every Sunday all the family met for tea at my grandparents' house. My grandfather taught me necessary skills: how to tip my tea into my saucer and blow waves across it until it was cool enough to drink; how to cut an orange in half crossways and pack a sugar lump into each half and then suck out orange-juice and sugar together; how to walk along the crazy-paving garden path without stepping on any of the cracks or a tiger would get you; how to butter the loaf and then clutch it to your chest and then shave off paper-thin slices; what saint to pray to when you woke up at night and saw the devil moving behind the curtains. We had shrimps for tea, watercress, celery stacked in a glass jug, fishpaste sandwiches, flan made from the blackberries hanging in thickets over the back garden fence from the wild common beyond. In April the garden was a jungle of bluebells, bursting from under the trees in blue tides above your ankles, but by midsummer my grandmother had it tame again, fifty yards of earth between wooden fences bearing docile rows of hollyhocks and sweet peas; an ex-army rug was spread on the shaven lawn for the children to sit on for tea outdoors.

After tea we children would wander off casually into the garage with despising giggles for the grownups planted solidly in their wicker chairs talking boring grown-up talk. We played the same game every Sunday; each one in turn pulled down his or her underwear and rotated slowly while the others watched. The fact that I knew it was wicked to expose my smooth bare slit gave me a feeling both of pleasure and of power, never vocalised. The game was carried on in silence.

'What about your school, though?' One of the women asked. Do you remember how, do you remember when, can you begin to realise why? And do you really want to?

I'm telling you a story, you remember that. Nostalgia for simple sensory experience cancels out the pain I didn't recognise then.

On our retreat in the last year of school, a visiting priest talked to us from Sister Superior's throne. The priest waved his arms up and down and exhorted us 'Be the angels of your homes'. For those with problems or vocations to be discussed, there were interviews in the convent parlour, hitherto sacrosanct. Most of us went, to savour talking to the man who abhorred women, in the forbidden room with its hard chairs and unopened windows and the heart bleeding over the door. The priest made us sit next to him on footstools; he bent his red face towards us and whispered that we should become the angels of our homes and his.

In that last summer term we spent a lot of time outdoors in the convent garden, in that part of it where our noisy unhallowed feet might tread. In our explorations, ostensibly in search of good compositions to sketch, we often came upon the nuns: a solitary sister on her knees in front of a grotto, a nervous magpie secreting days off purgatory, would fly up; a group of novices, disturbed roller-skating or playing the guitar, would look to their novice-mistress for permission to accept a boiled sweet.

I and my best friend Katy lay in the long grass below the tennis courts. The bell ringing the office was tinny on the warm air, the smell of mown grass was part of the heat of the afternoon, the fat ugly school dog Muffin wandered in search of Sister Superior's caresses.

'Are your parents coming to Open Day?' asked Katy through a mouthful of grass.

'My mother is.'

We lay back, our faces buzzing with heat and the noise of insects. We were practising for what we conceived of as adulthood. Our freedom that term: to lie and masturbate each other in the long grass below the tennis courts until the bell rang again, for the end of art class.

I did well at school because I was in love with and afraid of my teachers. A good essay meant a dry word of praise or an ironic look; not remembering theorems brought a turned back, sarcasm. Sister Paul would pretend not to see me as I hung about outside around the staffroom to see her pass by for the third time that day.

It took me a long time to learn to transfer my attention to men. But once at university I was an apt student. I learnt it, along with Old English grammar and D.H. Lawrence, another whole language of self-hatred and subservience.

Late afternoon, summer, the small suburban garden bloated with the marquee empty after my cousin's wedding and departure on honeymoon, my father's flushed face, my mother's face jerking, my own imminent departure back to Oxford, my head racing with wine and incense. I rang Peter from a callbox in Paddington station and asked if I could drop in to see him before going back. He understood me, was reassuring and only slightly bored.

The bottle of cheap wine empty, he kissed me expertly, then moved both our bodies onto the bed on the floor, a sheath tucked into his cheek in readiness.

I was embarrassed. The nuns and my mother, though schooling me well in the use of items such as forks, napkins, gloves, had omitted instructions on the manipulation of lips, arms, legs, cunt. These had always been kept closed, trussed-up, gingerly moved, kept out of the way lest they offend. Exposing them meant asking for it: whistles, pinches, rape. Now they were required to explode, dance, vibrate, arch, become continents crawling with armies of desire.

I lay back, stiff not with fear but with social embarrassment. Peter, finally noticing my immobility, ceased his busy efficient caresses and looked at me.

'D'you mean to tell me that this is the first time you've slept with anyone?' he asked incredulously. Ashamed, I could only nod. His actor's training came to his support. Giving me his most tender childlike smile he murmured, 'Well, what a very wonderful occasion,' and resumed his task. Five minutes later he flopped on top of me. Both our stomachs were set; a tiny trickle of blood on the sheet confirmed what I had not noticed: that I was no longer a virgin.

We slept. In the morning he was kind, fed me melon and wine on a pavement cafe in South Kensington, then pushed me onto a bus with a fatherly peck on the cheek, and went back to writing his play. I marched back to the flat past couples strolling damp and contented from the Cherwell boathouse. The north Oxford gardens were heavy with blossom, crowding sweetness along the roads, bushes of raindrenched lilac crouched behind stone walls, waiting for evening and release.

The chipped face of the Virgin, newly gaudy for Easter with pink and blue paint, stares detachedly|through Sister Martha: close half-sleeves to the elbow under the wide sleeves of her habit, kneelength stockings, large loose knickers doled out that morning from the heap in the laundry basket, lumpy sanitary towel strapped like a dead rabbit between her legs. A mild day, poached-egg clouds on a mottled sky like a face after crying, warm damp wind tossing the hair and skirts of bicyclists beyond the wall, the arms of trees. Sister Martha's father was a butcher in Fecamp years ago, his overall as blue as the habit she wears now. She paces the gravelled path between the redbrick walls of the kitchen garden, goosepimpled arms, legs and breasts under the serge tent, face frilled in white like a crown-roast cutlet. The novices empty vats of mutton scraps into the dustbins and pack them down with their bare hands. Her brother Claude creeps across to her bed in the middle of the night and strokes her toes. He served at mass every morning, you could see the muck on the soles of his boots. She was sometimes allowed to ring the little handbell at the elevation of the host. They had palms stuck behind the crosses above their beds; she used to get hers down and hold it when the man inside her bolster started trying to get out.

You were watching me steadily as I talked, listening, not saying very much. There were eight women at the meeting that night, sitting hunched about the room and on the floor. I knew I found it hard to remember they were there, was very aware of you as I talked. 'Go on,' you said as I stopped, 'go on.'

So I began to sleep with men in order to discover myself, to see, through their unknown, hitherto unmet eyes, the self that I really was at the same time as the self that I really might be. The confrontation involved in sex seemed of all those available to me for that purpose the most powerful, the most open, the most personal. But at the final moment, with a succession of lovers and of mirrors, vision distorted: I was presented with only a fractured picture of myself. That was how I perceived it, in wordless ways in my head, in my gut. Yet I did not know which to trust: the splintered yet separately concrete vision of myself each man offered me which was the product of his necessary fantasy; or the amorphous, difficult to establish whole self which struggled to say that his vision of me and mine through his, had distorted it. If I became part of his fantasy landscape a certain amount of security, great pleasure even, was possible, at the cost of feeling split and unknowable afterwards and unsure whether I as I felt I really was had experienced anything. If I did not trust and live his fantasy image of myself I could no longer reach out to distorted splinters and did not know where to begin to look for myself. I seemed to live two inches behind the front of my skin, that part of me created wilfully by my lovers. Certain parts of me were defined by the grass that I dented with my feet or the cushion that I hollowed with my back and had an identity both in time and space; but the breasts and cunt he briefly fondled existed only because touched at his will and through his perception of them. Poets plunged perpetually through thickets, climbed mountains, mapped new continents; whose were they, I wondered, where did they come from?

'Tell me,' I began to urge other women, 'what might be', and they to urge me.

The men who watched us began to feel uneasy. They hinted to all the women dependent on them in various ways that their shrill cries rendered them boring, humourless, sexually unappetising; they talked of castration by these same women and wept and offered themselves as small soft snails out of their snailshells to be cosseted back by mummy into strength and pleasure-giving. After a long day of wiping her son's eyes, arse and office floors, mummy was often too exhausted to continue the struggle.

My parents loved me without conditions, so they and all the stories told me; I seek a lover who will do the same. If you will not love me, having won me, I do not know who I am. I will be both the tiger in your back garden and the dove of your green jungle; Griselda under her disguise of ashes and ass's skin in your back kitchen and the radiant princess who reveals her lineage at your high table. I have learned to please, to gauge and sniff the air before I move off, to swing my head from side to side as I put one foot carefully in front of the other, ears and hair raised to twang on the slightest change in the atmosphere. This is the nature with which I desperately attune, knowing no other, with which I painfully harmonise, fearful always of the loss of the love which keeps me that way.

Self-hatred finally brought silence. One of the women pierced it in its tenderest place.

'Have you ever wanted to sleep with another woman?'

I couldn't answer that question because my thoughts were aimed at you, not at the painful roots of my current practice but at you, the conjuring of feelings by the spell and ritual of words, the seducing of you with poetry, I a peddlar tumbling stories before your dais. I began to recognise a landscape. I wanted to weep for an enormous violent sensuality I would never know again. The words tumbled out like machine gun fire.

My mother got married in black. Her punishment for wanting that English Protestant, my father, who proposed to her by telegram. Very keen marry you. It was wartime. They were punished together by the priest in black in the crypt of the French Catholic church in Leicester Square, its sombreness relieved only by Jean Cocteau's androgynous wall-paintings; they were allowed no flowers and no music. My mother wore a black suit with padded shoulders, a little hat over one eye, rolling shoulder curls, a hint of black veil. Afterwards they had a wedding breakfast in the Escargot restaurant in Greek Street nearby whose proprietor was an unofficial father figure to my mother so far away from home, and then they sent my mother's parents in Brittany a coded message via the free French radio: Marie is still eating snails and all is well. Marie is still within her father's house and all is well. Next day my father went back to the war and my mother back to the boarding school where she was on teaching practice as a French assistante, and spoke to the future wives of doctors and civil servants: Je suis, tu es, il est, nous sommes.

A romantic history, untouchable and unprovable and finally only consolatory, because my mother is dead. Dead before I knew it was not my anger killed her, dead before I told her how much I loved her.

That was when I started crying. Pity for myself, for the dislocation of my words, of the edifice carefully constructed to bury pain. Words, like death, like time or distance preserve love; fragrant as pot-pourri she scents my bed by night, my brain by day. She permeates me like scent in a room when the lid is lifted and the petals stirred, never a memory occasionally summoned but, so totally that I am unaware of it, forming the very fabric of the structure from which I gain my substance. So I cried in self-pity, and after watching me, you put your arms around me, as mothers and as lovers do.

You can't see down that part of the cloister leading off from the chapel into the convent. It goes straight for a few yards and then bends round the corner into blackness. They say there's a small garden there and a ten-foot high crucifix, they say that last Lent Sister Martha spent five hours in front of it every day. Sister Martha's hair shows under the drift of her veil, it's a dark cloud of seaweed around her pale and drowning face. The prettiest child in the first year holds her train, the Daughters of Mary, their medals on red cords around their necks, toss rose petals in front of the chaplain bearing his god-burden, hands wrapped in tangerine brocade, under a canopy with lurching gold fringes. Sister Martha's hair is cut off with a pair of gold scissors, she lies arms outflung on the marble slab. Her father, who is a butcher in Fecamp, has sent over the wedding breakfast for all the nuns and pupils: pate, garlic sausage and ham. There is a dead nun in the school chapel; Father gives the bridal sermon over my dead body.

My mother got married in black. There has been so much mourning to do.

I am the fountain sealed up, the walled garden where the lord Christ takes his rest at noon; I am my own grille and enclosure and the desperate bride vowed to him who blesses my chains. He enters me as fortress, I can only thank him from my battlements; I am the pearl the knight must capture to win heaven and the drug that will detain him from his quest. I am always and everywhere his place; if I am the barren land he thinks to water into an oasis I am also the blight on his crops and the locust destroying grain; I am both the ruined harvest and the shameful blood that sickens cattle.

And so I'm crying now; it's five o'clock and you'll be arriving any minute. My own tears, hot noisy gulping that burns and blotches, that neither you nor any of the women in the group is going to offer to staunch, tears of anger for myself and all of us, anger with the women in the group for making me face up to what I'm doing to you, for making me want to take out those dusty bundles of old stories from where they've lain for my lifetime tied up with pink ribbon and reread them and throw them away.

Traitor goddess. Whore madonna. Bitch sister. Someone I've dreamed of and whom I'm going to work with. Whose equal vulnerability once frightened me, whose equal violence gladdens me. You've arrived wearing a black suit with padded shoulders and a whole garden pinned to your lapel. We discuss the abortion struggle for a long time. We speak with effort and with care, trusting each other equally to climb alone across the clumsy stepping-stones of words, no longer corpses in the church and mouths of men.

The Freedom of Rosemary Patan
(*As told to Valerie Miner*)

'Oh, shit! If I hear that line about "sisterly support" once more!' said Rosemary. 'Look, "feminism" isn't just a convenient emotional placenta.'

She wasn't angry at the old woman from Bath. She didn't know who to blame. She felt splintered between rage and despair at — *at these same bloody words* she had heard for the past seven years. The same women's workshops held in the same baroque auditoria and green primary classrooms. She had come to England to find the roots of the Women's Movement and found them stunted in the same self-conscious discussions she heard all over North America. No, that was unfair. She believed in conferences like this which brought together women from all stages of the movement. She still believed in consciousness-raising exercises. But some people forgot why they were exercising.

The old woman looked confused, glanced down at her knit skirt and smoothed the wrinkles between the peach and avocado stripes. She smiled ironically at the ten other women sitting on the metal folding chairs in the stuffy classroom. 'But surely,' she cleared her throat, 'we all need support to. . . .'

'There are too many ways,' interrupted Rosemary, 'to exploit the Women's Movement for plain selfish reasons.' She steadied herself on the penmanship exercise over the blackboard. 'You can't just sit back grooving on the sisterly vibes.'

Rosemary knew she shouldn't be angry at these women. She recited the litany to herself, 'Blessed Susan B. Anthony, Agnes McPhail, Olive Schreiner, Emmeline Pankhurst. . . .' She could feel Rowena's foot pressing against hers. 'Relax.' She had often put people off with this 'North American vigour'. Even back home her quixotic commitment seemed an admonition.

The old woman shook her head resolutely. '*First*, you have to feel strong in yourself.'

'Anyway,' said the moderator, 'everyone here has put herself on the line except you. It's your turn to tell a consciousness-raising story or do you think the exercise is too individualistic and contrived?'

'OK, OK,' she laughed. 'But I don't go in for all this romantic personal narrative stuff. We have to be careful about "literary form" being too patriarchal. Also, this objective "third person". . . .'

'Enough pedantic waffling,' said the Newcastle delegate.

'Let's get on with it,' cheered the Scot. 'You're the one who's been talking about *action* and analysis.'

'Right,' said Rosemary. 'Shall we imagine the front page of a Canadian radical newspaper, you all know the sort, with dripping red logo and grey, grey photos of the prisoners of society:

FREE PATAN
SMASH REPRESSION
by an Evedaughter

She turned and faced the courtroom, 'I have nothing to say for myself. It has all been said for me.'

Rosemary Patan, today was convicted of exhibiting a disgusting object, wilful damage and assault causing bodily harm. Throughout her three-week trial, she refused to testify on her own behalf. In solidarity with her contempt of the fascist Canadian courts, the Canadian Alliance of Women Socialists (CAWS) has called a rally and march to follow our sister from the Newman Police Station to the Don Jail.

This is the last in a series of indepth features on the struggle of Rosemary Patan. The research was done during the trial and afterward in Patan's cell. We chose this personal issue because we believe that Patan's oppression is a useful paradigm. Although CAWS objects to the bourgeois romanticism of her unaligned tactic, we must defend her commitment to radical feminism.

Her demonstration with the life-size photographs of the casualties of back-street abortions outside the Ontario Parliament Buildings was a cause celebre among the established Movement. Separatists were barred from the courtroom which was heavy with liberal credentials. Witnesses included the defendant's sister, prominent gynaecologist Pat Patan and Sister Rose Sullivan, Professor of Women's Studies at St Michael's College. The defence attorney was Mary Hammer whose impassioned democratic oratory has pegged her as a potential NDP candidate.

Meanwhile, the whole issue of abortion was coopted into an harangue about democratic debate. Judge Simpson held that free speech did not entitle one to abuse public property. Patan was fined $200 for damage to the base of Queen Victoria's statue where she had chained herself.

Patan was as private in her cell as she had |been in| the dock. She denied the anti-imperialist significance of her action, admitting only that it was a reaction to six years' futility within the abortion campaign. She made no rebuttal to those on the Left — CAWS, RMG, YS and even the CP — who charged that her protest was a counterproductive emotional self-indulgence.

Indeed, Patan can be seen as a model of liberal politicisation. As we sat in her cramped cell listening to the pigs rattling poker chips upstairs, I asked why she refused to join a revolutionary group. 'I have,' she insisted, 'the Women's Movement.' This is the extent of her analysis.

Patan ignores the broader implications of the abortion issue, concerned only with changing one law. She ignores the evidence of working class oppression as well as the police repression exposed in recent abortion demonstrations. She says simply, 'I'll join the vanguard to control society when we have the right to control our own bodies.'

We must be careful not to make her a heroine. For many of us, this tough, perseverant woman was the inspiration to feminism. I personally met Patan on the 1970 march and walked proudly behind her 'Free Abortion on Demand' banner. But this issue is *not* as separate as she would try to convince us. We must take her struggle one step further.

Sisters and brothers are urged to help smash sexist and classist legislation at Saturday's demonstration, starting at 1pm at the Newman Police Station. The rally at the Don Jail will include speakers from CLM, RMG, YS as well as CAWS. Come add your voice to *Free Rosemary Patan*.

Rosemary breathed deeply and regarded the other women in the classroom. They watched her expectantly, all except the old woman who said, 'I sympathise with your "struggle" — yes, I think it is a struggle. But I worry about all this exhibitionism. Anyway,' she said quickly, aware that this was an unpopular tactic, 'it's not much of a story, is it? So dry and polemical and one-sided.'

'Absolutely,' said Rosemary. 'Shall I continue?' Her voice grew more personal, quieter. 'Think of a cold May afternoon.'

From the street below, only one cell of the police station seemed to be occupied. Pat Patan saw the figure of a bulky young man, the straight brown hair straggling to the collar of the beige sports jacket. An alcoholic hard-hat or a thug, maybe a plainclothes policeman. But she knew it was her sister Rosemary. Rosemary, hunched and tense, trying to ignore the smell of horseshit from the stable and the rattling of the poker chips upstairs. Rosemary reading or writing one of her Marxist texts.

Pat remembered Rosemary running up these slippery grey steps when they were kids, playing tag on the way home from St Paul's. No-one dared follow. She warned Rosemary — twenty-five years ago — that she would get locked up if she kept behaving like *that*.

'Ms Patan, please.'

'Upstairs, lady, in the Bridal Suite.'

She winced, less irritated by the sergeant's sarcasm than by what it predicted about Rosemary's mood. By now she should be used to the effect of her sister's tempers on the rest of humanity. She had defended Rosemary's right to join the football team, although she couldn't understand why she wanted to be a tomboy. Gradually, she too, became keen on sport and followed Rosemary's progress through high school with an excellent track record of her own. Pat had explained to their parents why Rosemary wanted to divorce the American draft resister three years after she had explained why Rosemary wanted to marry him. And that had decided Pat, herself, against wifery.

'Ms Patan,' she said, slurring the 'Ms' and hating herself for lacking Rosemary's imperviousness. 'Ms' was simple enough: why did she pretend to be slurring 'Miss' or 'Mrs'. The West Indian guard considered her with remote curiosity. Not the usual sort of visitor.

'That's exactly what I mean,' said the old woman. She smiled at the new speaker who averted her glance of complicity. Then she turned to Rosemary with more reproach than she intended, 'You don't have to make a big militant show to be a feminist.'

'By your definition,' said the Scot, 'maybe the Virgin Mary was a feminist?'

'Hey, hey, I thought this was *my* story,' said Rosemary. 'If I can bring you back to Toronto a couple of weeks later, inside a courtroom sanctioned by your Queen and mine.'

'My client refuses to enter a plea because she was simply exercising her democratic right to self-expression when she assembled her placards around the statue of Queen Victoria at the Ontario Parliament Buildings. My client. . . .'

Mary turned to find her client reading a worn hardback book under the table. The least she could do is pay attention. Even as her lawyer, it was hard to maintain empathy with Rosemary's insolent posture and attire. She might make some concessions to the politics of the court.

Mary was still stinging from the ruckus Rosemary made about having a woman lawyer. Honest-to-fucking Jesus, Rosemary had gone too far. She had called John a phallic opportunist. John, of all people who had allocated an extra thousand dollars to the Equality Fund.

Mary appreciated the need for solidarity. She finally accepted the case because Rosemary was *her* cause. Mary had never really *identified* with the Ojibways in that Northern Ontario summer or the Italians during that field term on College Street. She was never *part* of the community. She felt like a sociological exploiter. She gave up union law because the auto workers' picket line made her feel like another trendy liberal. They just weren't *her* issues. The Women's Movement was home after all that. She could identify with the arguments and the individuals. But she wasn't a separatist. Unlike Rosemary, she distinguished between liberation and vituperation.

'My client maintains that her protest was no more sensational than the placards of magnified fetuses carried by the Right-to-Life Campaign. Furthermore, my client believes her twenty-four-hour vigil would have passed peaceably if four members of that organisation had not threatened her and forcibly removed her posters.'

Rosemary had done a creditable job with them, four men being no match for one woman's Aikado. But she would ignore the heroics since Rosemary had started the fight. This separatist thing had to be avoided. She hated to pull 'professional' rank on Rosemary, but she had requested a closed gallery. She would have no chance with a feminist rooting section in the back of the courtroom.

In fact, she had been warned about her own rhetoric, not befitting a member of the Bar. But it was hard to hold back when you finally had a case you believed in. Her senior partners didn't mind the publicity. Their firm had a 'political' reputation. John and Peter started with Vietnam deserters a few years ago; now it was mostly West Indian immigrants. It was a cooperative practice where they gave her a lot of freedom, asking only that she cut down the rhetoric.

'This particular statute has been attacked in all the major papers by clergymen, teachers, government officials. Her protest was, I submit, wholly within the tradition of free speech. My client's efforts can only be viewed as another flank in the same campaign . . . .'

Admittedly, it wasn't the *same* campaign. Rosemary called for free abortion on demand. But one made compromises in oratory, for the larger truth, for the client's welfare. She hoped Rosemary would let it pass. Putting a hand on her client's shoulder, she assumed a more authoritative tone,

'Ms Patan was appointed to the Royal Commission on the Status of Women. . . .'

She omitted that Rosemary resigned immediately and that for the past two years had made less formal contributions, like running her own unlicensed vacuum aspiration clinic. One made compromises. Oratory. Yes, several people had commented on Mary's skill. Poised and forthright. Sometimes she thought she'd like to run, maybe as an independent women's candidate. Maybe with the NDP.

'My client's actions should not be censured, but rather applauded. We all have a lot to learn from the courage and conviction of Rosemary Patan.'

'Bloody bourgeois opportunist,' said the Scot. 'You can see she's just using the case to further her own career.'

'Now, is that quite fair?' asked the moderator-catalyst. 'Isn't she risking a lot by taking on the issue?'

'Oh, hell she is. Radical chic. Radical chic makes me sick. That's all that sort of protest is — cocktail conversation for the radical chic.'

'Hold on a minute,' said Rosemary. 'Let me finish the story:

She was really the same Rosemary when you came right down to it, the same pudgy girl who stood up in grade three and demanded, 'If God is all powerful, does that mean he could make someone more powerful and then he wouldn't be all powerful anymore? Anyway, why's God a Him?'

Then, Sister Rose had been more intrigued by the girl's first question. But she never forgot the second. In those days, she didn't know how to doubt holy masculinity. You didn't even question the length of the habit.

'I have known Rosemary Patan, first as a young pupil and subsequently as a friend, for twenty-three years.' Sister Rose was a small woman whose quick, deliberate hand movements camouflaged the nervousness in her voice. All very well to teach women's studies at St Michael's, to be called 'Sister Libby'. Quite another thing to be character witness for an abortion campaigner. If there was one lesson she had taught Rosemary and Rosemary had taught her, it was to defend one's beliefs.

'Rosemary was always a precocious child. I remember once in a history lesson — she was only eight at the time — she asked what was wrong with witches after all? "They just seem to say wise things — like the prophets — how come they burned them?"'

Sister regarded the judge's set expression and offered up another anecdote. 'She used to want to be a nun. She prayed very hard for a vocation. She was never very good at meditation, but when she was in junior high she joined the Sodality and went around the yard at recess, dragging kids into church to say the rosary. You see, she's always been a bit of an apostle. I'm sure she would have made a fine bishop if — if things were different.'

Sister Rose's voice grew more confident with the testimony. Better stick to topic, she admonished herself. 'Rosemary was a devout child, with the largest collection of holy cards in class. Saint Teresa of Avila was her favourite as I recall. Anyway, there was a great crisis of conscience when Sister Ann Amanda scolded her for winning them all at Bingo.'

She was pleased to see Rosemary laugh now. It was the first sign of her involvement in the trial. Sister Rose hadn't talked to her for months, ever since that argument about whether to call her book a 'Feminist Christian Analysis' or a 'Christian Feminist Analysis'. The last time they had seen each other, Rosemary had been standing at the back of chapel listening to Sister Rose's homily. When Sister looked for Rosemary after Mass, she had vanished.

'I don't think it's heretical in 1976 to suggest that there is a correlation between religious conviction and political commitment. Nor do I claim it

as an original observation that the Convent is the epitome of sisterhood
— of "feminism" if you like — of women working together and supporting each other.'

She noticed that Rosemary was looking down, jotting something in a
book under the table.

'Of course, Rosemary and I have our philosophical differences, the
abortion issue being one of them. Although I don't sanction abortion, I
have taught the concept of free will long enough so that I support a
woman's right to make her own decisions.' She considered the faces
around the courtroom as she said this, wondering what her superior
would say when she read the newspapers. But then, who were you
without the courage of your conviction?

'I still rely on her challenging conversation and, sometimes,' she
smiled fondly, 'confrontation. I have asked her to lecture to several of my
classes. I firmly believe her action can only be judged as a genuine
statement of conscience.'

She stepped down from the stand with the relief of one absolved and
nodded to Rosemary, confident in their conspiracy.

The women in the green classroom waited for Rosemary to continue.

'Well, that's it,' she said.

The woman from Northampton was considering her cuticles and the
Scot was formulating a position as the old woman blurted, 'But that's not
your short story. That's not *it*?'

'It's a story and it's short, isn't it?'

'I mean, well, I mean, well, ummmmmhow long were you in jail?'

'Just two months. They let me out on parole when I started trying to
organise a prisoners' union.'

'And now,' asked the Scot, 'are you cynical about the Women's
Movement?'

'What good would that be?'

'So you're still an active feminist?' asked the old woman.

'Oh, yes.'

'What do you do in the Movement?'

'I write stories.'

Keep It Clean
Michelene Wandor

The following fragment of a manuscript is the third in our series 'Women: 50 years ago'. It was found among a collection of magazines, news-sheets and leaflets which were sent to us by one of the researchers for our archives on feminism in the 20th century. The fragment was accompanied by a letter, dated March 10, 1991, from 'Annie' to 'Sheila'. The two women met at the International Women's Day March, after a break in their friendship of twenty years. Annie recalls, in fictional form, the event which led to the rift in their friendship, apparently referring to herself in the third person.

Regular readers will recall that the first half of the 1970s saw an unprecedented upsurge of feminist activism, the most vigorous since the struggle for the vote in the first two decades of the century. Following the fragment is the first in our series chronicling the origins, the political range of what was then called the Women's Liberation Movement. The fragment sheds some illumination on what it was like to be a feminist 50 years ago, though we would point out that it was written 20 years after the event with all the problems of interpretation that implies. If readers have any other memoirs, stories, conference notes of the period, we would be grateful for them. After being recorded on film they will be returned.

We do not know if the fragment was ever sent to 'Sheila'.

(Editorial Board: *History Lives*, October 2026)

(...*benefit of hindsight. Of course, it was all too immediate, though some of us kept diaries; now we select and interpret looking back from a different personal life and a very different political time*.)

Annie and Sheila perched side by side on a high window-sill, their feet resting on a table on which three other women sat. From the walls framed aldermen stared blandly down at the gathering of some five hundred local people, mostly women, mostly in their twenties and thirties.

A line of people filed onto the stage: Annie and Sheila split a roll of mints, and waved to other women they recognised. It was the third in a series of six meetings on women's liberation, organised by the women's group in the local Polytechnic. 1971, it was. The chairperson adjusted the microphone. The assembly whispered into silence: she welcomed everyone, introduced the people on the stage, including two members of the local Trades Council who had helped sponsor the meetings, and introduced the evening's main speaker, Lesley Wright.

Lesley walked to the microphone as the chairperson retreated from it to a spatter of applause. Lesley surveyed the audience, her shock of blonde permed hair catching the light, her denim jeans and combed cotton T-shirt a kind of individual permutation on the unofficial 'uniform' of the younger, higher-educated feminism. She pushed the microphone aside, and began to speak in a firm voice, used to public speaking, hands leaning forward on the table, one occasionally raised to emphasise a point.

'Sisters. Ours is a powerful movement. All over the world we are rising up and refusing the exploited identity for which we were conditioned.

'As women we are forced to accept that if we have a relationship with a man, it will involve a lot of work: looking after him, putting his needs before ours. Even if both man and woman are earning a wage, the man's wage will be higher than the woman's and so his job more important than the woman's. If we want children, then our wage will stop when the children are young and we are home fulltime. We will have to depend on the father for money or else scrape by on Social Security. The wife and mother who goes out of the home to earn a wage, to escape being totally dependent on a man, being isolated in the home, and the penny-pinching that trying to make one wage feed the family involves, takes a second job. And even if we don't marry or live with a man, the fact that most women do means that every man will see a housewife when he sees us. Men expect us to be at their disposal sexually and emotionally. To be sympathetic to their problems, bolster their egos, have a ready smile, care for their children, make the tea.

'*All women are housewives*. Single or married, young or old, with or without children, lesbian or straight, that housework is our first job. We are saying that government and employers — the State owes us a living. Men and women work all day and at the end of the week those in waged work get a wage packet which doesn't buy much more than the necessities of life. Those who have worked at home get nothing. The wealth that we have created goes to the employers and the State. Our housework goes on behind the scenes, unnoticed, uncounted, uncharted as long as it is unpaid. We demand that our work should be recognised for what it is — we produce and reproduce in other people and ourselves the ability to work and go on working, we produce labour power. All other production would grind to a halt tomorrow if women weren't producing these workers.

'What we want is very simple: we want wages for housework. It is not a new idea, and it is the only demand around which all women can unite, the demand which makes explicit how it is that the working class is divided between the waged and the unwaged. Money is power in our society; give us a wage for our housework, and then we will have power.'

A burst of applause from the middle of the hall; Sheila clapping energetically, her hands held high in front of her; Annie, confused, somewhat anxious, a knot of surprise at Sheila's enthusiasm. Something she couldn't quite articulate, an intuitive hostility to both the arguments and the conclusions they had just heard. The chairperson was back, Lesley seated to her right. She invited questions, responses to 'a very interesting speech'. A man stood up:

'I'm not really for all this women's lib business, but I go for what this young lady says. My wife'd be a lot better off if she was getting a proper wage for her housework, then she'd have to bloody well do it properly.' Women round him started heckling — 'She's a woman, not a young lady', 'When did you last boil an egg'. The man began to retreat towards the door under the hail — 'I'm with you, girls, I want my wife to get a wage; then if she don't do her work, she don't get paid — like me.' As he reached the door, with a variety of helpful obstructions he shouted his Parthian shot — 'You can't bloody have it both ways. . . '

'Good riddance,' shouted Sheila. Annie nudged her, whispering: 'Isn't it a gross over-simplification to say the working class is just divided between the waged and the unwaged?' 'Pedant, Annie,' said Sheila happily. 'Great, isn't she?'

Annie stood up on the table. 'I'm going,' she said to Sheila.

'See you later,' said Sheila, already half listening to the next question. '. . . wages for housework is the only thing that unites women. After all, isn't that a rejection of the complexity of women's oppression? We can't just reduce the struggles of half the population to a demand for money. Anyway, wouldn't it come out of taxation?'

Lesley stood to reply: 'Let me explain. Wages for housework. . . '

The swing doors shut behind Annie. As she walked down the wide stone steps to the ground floor her confusion was diverted by the sight of two men in their twenties, chatting together and keeping a watchful early evening eye over two three-year-olds playing hide and seek round the curve of the banisters.

(*. . . sorry I've got to go, sorry I'm late, sorry I'm so pretty, sorry I'm a housewife, sorry I'm not pretty enough, sorry it's my fault, pardon me for breathing, sorry I'm a woman. We did stop apologising, didn't we?*)

When Annie got home, Mike was sprawled over the couch watching telly. She went straight into the kitchen, and automatically made them both a cup of coffee, a mutual family ritual when one of them went out

to a meeting. He patted the arm of the couch as she came in, but she
ignored it, sitting on the floor, and absent-mindedly collecting bits of
crushed crisp off the carpet into one hand.

The credits came up and Mike switched the TV off. 'Well?'

'Kids all right?'

'Fine. A fight over a car, but otherwise calm.'

'Good.'

'Well?'

'Well, what?'

'Well, how was the meeting?'

'Oh, all right.'

'Was that the meeting about women and the family?'

'Supposed to be. This woman talked about housework.'

'How to get hubby to do the washing up?'

Mike trying to cover up his unease about staying in so she could go out
by patronising sarcasm. Annie couldn't be bothered to spell out his
response for him to become aware of. 'Wages for housework, that's what
she suggested; good safe economist demand. Should be right up your
street.' Matching sarcasm with sarcasm didn't really help, it just made
you feel momentarily better.

'I've heard of them,' said Mike. 'They've put out a pamphlet, haven't
they?'

'I don't know. Why didn't you bloody tell me?'

'I've hardly seen you this evening, have I? Saw it in the People's
Bookshop window on the way home. "Wages for Housework" it's
called.'

'Well, they're up the creek.' Annie picked up her half-full coffee mug
and flounced into the kitchen, suddenly at bay. She poured the coffee
down the sink, then started running hot water to wash up the supper
dishes. Mike followed her in.

'Leave it, Annie, I'll do it in the morning.'

'Bullshit. You've got to be at school by quarter to nine in the morning.
I'll do it in the morning. Except I won't because I hate doing damn
dishes in the morning.'

Mike gently pulled her away from the sink and began washing up.
Annie allowed him, irritated at his apparent calm. She wiped the top of
the stove to give her something to do.

'It was bloody awful. Screwy sort of argument — I mean, what she was
really saying was half right on the nail, and half like a whirlpool that
sucks everything into it.'

'How do you mean?'

'Well, she said a lot of good things about how housework and things
were essential *social* work — you know, saying it was work, hard work,

servicing other people, not that airy fairy labour of love stuff, and how it ought to be recognised, and how it was because women were seen as wives and mothers that they got low wages, no money when they were at home looking after small kids. And then she kind of jumped into this absurd thing of suddenly saying that meant that all women were housewives, and that wages for housework was the thing that united all women.'

'What did she mean by a wage?'

'Just money. I'm afraid I got very annoyed and left; it was pretty obvious to me that there wasn't going to be a proper discussion.'

'Did her whole group come?'

'What a suspicious mind you've got.'

'Tactics, Annie. No-one's above tactics.'

'Someone was beginning to ask about women as wage-earners when I left. I imagine the wages for housework people must think that any work by women in the unions is a waste of time. By definition women are first and only housewives. And yet it is true in a way that women have two jobs. . .'

'87 per cent of women work at some time in your lives.'

'Lucky us, eh?'

'And some of us men are learning to take a second job, eh?'

'Learning's a matter of opinion.'

'Right. Coming to bed?' Mike dried his hands on the tea-towel. Annie nodded and automatically went over to the sink to check that everything was done. With a rush of fury she picked up the J-cloth which was sitting in a pool of greasy water at the bottom of the sink. 'And what's this?'

'What?'

'This.' Holding up the cloth.

'That,' said Mike, 'is a J-cloth. Now come to bed.'

'You don't bloody notice when we've run out, do you?'

Neither of them slept particularly well that night.

(Remember the good bits?)

Annie was putting the baby's night nappy on. A towelling nappy, and nappy liner. He was in a rosy mood, kicking his legs and grabbing at her hands as she tried to get the material firmly round his podgy middle. When she manouevred her hands out of his reach he would suddenly arch his back, straighten his legs, dig his heels into the bed and twist his body vigorously to the left, trying to get free of those firm, busy hands. He was still small and malleable enough for Annie to put the palm of her hand over his chest and tummy, swing him back onto his back and tickle him gently with the tips of her splayed fingers. Alex giggled deep down in his stomach and his arms and legs met like a soft anemone over her hand in an attempt to come to terms with it. Annie felt her hand enclosed in a warm cocoon of talcum powder and smooth baby skin.

As Annie adjusted the nappies under the wriggling body, she glossed back over the previous week. Unusually for her and Sheila, they had had no contact with each other. Their local women's group had met the day after the public meeting, and Sheila and Annie had had a fierce argument; Sheila had been enthusiastic, Annie icy and antagonistic to the idea of wages for housework. The argument had in effect been adjourned to this week, during which time the group was to read and digest the pamphlets Sheila had brought along. Annie had an uneasy sense of premonition, a kind of dread in her stomach at the prospect of this evening's meeting. She and Sheila had had disagreements before — not really surprising when you'd known someone for twelve years, since the first day they had peered at the college noticeboard together. The two of them had been virtually inseparable — periods of separation coinciding with the respective presences of boy-friends; even though Sheila had left university abruptly in her second year, hating the academic competitiveness. Where Annie had got an average degree, taught English 'O' Level, married Mike and had Sally and Alex, settling in London, Sheila had sailed close to the fringes of student politics in the late 1960s, been arrested for demonstrations against the American presence in Vietnam in the war which ended in the early 1970s, squatted with the squatters, and done a variety of part-time nomadic jobs. The last few years they had been more apart, until in 1969 they both rediscovered each other in one of the first Women's Liberation groups in London. The group had been meeting for two years, and it was mainly a consciousness-raising group, although, with only about twenty groups in London as a whole, some of them, the 'housewives', the women who worked part-time were also able to help run the voluntary rota in the central London office, the Women's Liberation Workshop.

It was all very well letting the panorama of London feminism run through your head, but meanwhile Alex had decided he didn't like thoughts. He squirmed, and the safety-pin, almost clasped, flew open and onto the floor. As Annie bent to retrieve it her face came in line with Alex's rosy bottom. As the nappy fell apart, a rich brown revelation mingled itself with the scent of talcum powder.

'Oh, shit, Alex,' she said. Alex giggled in anticipation of more fun and games. 'You don't know which end is up, do you, piggy?' she said, wiping his bottom with the clean nappy and then with it in one hand and Alex under the other arm she went back into the bathroom. She sluiced down the lower half of his body in the bath, rinsed the nappy and carried him back into the bedroom. This time he sensed the determination behind her hands and played with a rag book as she put a new nappy on him.

Now simply efficient, she finished dressing him, put him into his cot and handed him his final bottle of milk of the day. He held up his arms for a kiss and she melted into a sleepy hug and kiss, during which he had the final word and spluttered dribble against her cheek. She tickled him briefly, making him fold sitting into the cot. 'Night, night, fatty boy.' 'Ni, ni,' said Alex, already slurping into his bottle.

Annie was going to be late. She hurried through the living room, picking up her bag, coat, pamphlet as she went. She kissed Mike and Sally; he was sitting in a huge armchair, looking through the notes for his radical teachers' group meeting, Sally sitting quietly on his lap. After a year of experiment she and Mike had agreed that where both of them had meetings on the same night, Mike would try and arrange his at home: he could listen and take part in a discussion with a two-year-old on his lap. Annie couldn't.

(*This is the hard bit. Can you ever remember all the second-by-second nuances, points of view, movements in a single evening, let alone a generation? In how many ways have we written our history?*)

The front door to the house was ajar. Annie rang the top bell and then went to the third floor, Susan's flat.

(*Remember the group? Originally nine of them, now six, skip this if their images are as stamped in your mind as they are in mine. But it was a fairly typical group of its time.*
Susan: 27. Left school at 17 when she got pregnant, married, now separated, with two kids. In her first year at teacher-training college, her older sister looks after her kids after school, but can't baby-sit in the evenings. The meetings hence always at Susan's.
Ruth: 21. Serious, rarely smiles, sociology student at the local polytechnic. Father a miner, mother dead. In Annie's own youth Ruth would have been a swat in suburbia.
Jennifer: 26, had a variety of white-collar jobs, now in her second year of training to be a State Registered Nurse. Had had trouble being accepted for training — they said she was 'over-qualified'. Shared a house with other people; was gay but so far reticent about discussing it in such a predominantly heterosexual group.
Rachel: 33, married to a long-distance lorry driver, twins, worked mornings in a local cafe, probably the only member of the group who would define both her family history and her own current social position as unequivocally 'working class'. Born and brought up in the area, unlike other members of the group who had lived locally for periods of one to seven years.)

Sheila: *30, London suburban background, now squatting, helping to set up a law centre to advise women. No children.*
Annie: *31, English teacher in a comprehensive school, part-time, two children, married to Mike, primary school teacher full-time. Apart from times when one of them was out at work, they tried to share housework and child-care between them.*)

Rachel was usually the last to arrive, but tonight Annie found she was the last. People were sitting on chairs, the floor, drinking coffee and chatting, various newsletters and pamphlets on the floor in the middle. Annie picked up her copy of the Workshop weekly newsletter and skimmed down the list of meetings, appeals for information, contacts, list of new women's liberation publications.

Susan came in, flustered, her youngest with tooth-ache, she said, but now with Junior Disprin hopefully off to sleep. There was a small silence; then Jennifer asked a question about one of the meetings listed for next week in the area. Then another small silence.

Annie began to feel a surge of impatience. One of the important elements in the small 'consciousness-raising' group had been the principle of a non-hierarchical structure and form for discussion. This, everyone had agreed two years back, was because women were so used to being in groups dominated by a minority of articulate men (all groups — social, work, political) that it was important they (we) should be able to discover and articulate our own understanding of all the minute day-by-day ways in which we were oppressed, and relate these to a developing understanding of the ways women were oppressed in society generally. The exploration of our own personal experiences, and the linking up of these to an understanding that the isolated experience of individual women was part of a more complex system of female subordination. We want to break away from the way men behave, not imitate them. In practice, of course, this often resulted in one or two women talking too much in a meeting, 'dominating', it was called. It meant some women sat in virtual silence, unable to speak, even in the relative security of women's groups. The group had had numerous discussions about whether or not they should have a rotating chairperson, some people arguing fiercely that we shouldn't imitate male structures, that we were developing genuinely new ways of relating, conducting political discussions; we must all learn to be more sensitive, not interrupt each other, not talk for too long. Everyone would nod. Others in the group argued that up to a point all those things were right, but that often a subject was complex, often it could be constructive for everyone to have a chairperson who would guide discussion, not control it, who would be able to be supportive when someone talked too much or too little. We should develop or modify existing structures as well as work out new ones. Everyone would nod.

The result was an uneasy compromise, in which for some meetings there would be a chairperson, in others not. It depended on whether one of the pro-chairperson people suggested it. Tonight, surprisingly, Annie thought, it was Rachel who said 'Let's have a chair, eh?'

Susan: Do we need one?

Rachel: I reckon it'll help. Sheila and Annie did go on a bit last time.

Ruth: Jenny, will you do it?

Jenny: OK. I'm not very good, though.

In response to a question Sheila described the South London women's group who had produced the pamphlet arguing for wages for housework. She had been to one of their meetings, and was even more confirmed not only in the conviction that they were right, but that her own group should get involved in trying to organise women to campaign for wages for housework.

Sheila: We've spent two years meeting, talking, going to other meetings, we should get involved in doing something practical.

Annie: We do all do some other political things, Sheila.

Sheila: But not as a group. We're becoming a kind of hen-party.

Ruth: I don't think that's an accurate description of us, Sheila.

Sheila: Well, perhaps I didn't mean it quite like that. The thing that hit me, really hit me, was that they are the first group who have really said anything serious, analytical, about housework. I mean, we all wrote loads and loads of stuff saying what a drag housework was, how trapped women were in their kitchens, but no-one's analysed it before, and no-one's had any ideas about what to do about it. They want to make housework recognised and valued for what it is — necessary social labour.

Annie: And they say the whole system would collapse if women didn't do housework.

Sheila: Right.

Annie: What about if all the power workers, you know, gas, electricity, coal even, what if they all went on strike.

Susan: What do you mean, Annie?

Annie: It isn't only women, it isn't only housework that's necessary social labour.

Sheila: But only housework doesn't have a wage, only housework isn't really thought of as work, only housework is despised, and only women do housework.

Rachel: Oh come off it, Sheil, I know men who do housework.

Sheila: Yes, they 'help'.

Rachel: No, no, I mean blokes who live on their own, men who help, men who do other work about the house, even if it isn't cleaning and that. And you can't say that a woman on her own, going out to work, with no kids, just doing for herself, is a housewife like say I'm a housewife.

Sheila: But that's what we're all brought up to be.

Rachel: Yes, well, that is right, we are, mainly.

Susan: But what Sheila says is right, isn't it? I mean you say 'I'm only a housewife', and then some man comes home and thinks you've done fuck-all all day. They never see what you've done, do they? I mean, it's all invisible. They come home to a nice bathed kid and they don't know how much shit you've wiped up during the day. . .

Rachel: Yes, but I don't think you can just say all women are housewives. Because I don't think wages for housework is the same thing as saying that when women have to give up their jobs when their kids are little, or if there aren't no nurseries, that they should have bigger family allowances, that isn't the same as saying wages for housework, is it?

Susan: Well, you needn't call it wages for housework, you could call it the state paying for childcare at home, couldn't you?

Ruth: Sue, that does seem to me a very different issue from wages for housework.

Sheila: But all women do do housework, don't we, whether we're with guys or not.

Rachel: You must be pretty gormless if you go on doing your boyfriend's washing, is all I can say. With kids it's different. With men you tell 'em to do their own or go smelly. You don't want to get paid for doing it and them still not do it. I think I'll get Fred to wash his own overalls. See what it's like.

Sheila: But you've only got a job in the mornings.

Rachel: Yes, that's true. Well, he can iron his best shirts. That's it. I'll teach him to iron his shirts.

Ruth: Children are dependent. And that's why it is wrong for women to be financially penalised when they have children. But surely what we want is more than just housework to be waged and left as it is? We want to be able to challenge the whole idea of housework being women's work, just as we want to challenge whether engineering or surgery or being a crane driver or a football referee, whether any of those are men's jobs.

Sheila: Men won't value housework until it's paid.

Ruth: But look, Sheila. Women are not vulnerable just because they do housework. What I mean is, women are vulnerable when they are housewives because they also have sole responsibility for childcare at home. Do you see what I mean? I mean, with women getting equal pay, *when* women get equal pay, when there are things like adequate maternity leave and women don't lose their jobs because they have kids, and when there are enough nurseries —

Sheila: When, when, when. Wages for housework bypasses all those other struggles — well, I mean, with wages for housework, women wouldn't have to go out and take a second job.

Rachel: You're joking. I go round the bend just looking after kids all day. Whether I bloody got paid for it or not. If I want to have a job looking after kids, I'll get one in a nursery, or learn to be a teacher. Even if I was paid twice what I get at the cafe, I still wouldn't bloody stick at home all day.

Sheila: But don't you want the choice?

Rachel: No, thank you. I'd have liked the choice of a nursery when they were little, but you know, in a way now I have got the choice. I only work part of the week, well, for money. Then I am at home when the kids get in from school. I like that, yes. I think we want more part-time jobs, properly paid, not slave labour.

Jennifer: 'You don't get me, I'm part of the union?'

Rachel: That's right, that's right.

Sheila: When did the unions last get off their arses to do anything for women? Who runs the unions? It's men, isn't it? Men who want their wives at home.

Jennifer: But there's an Equal Pay Act that's supposed to come into force at the end of 1975 — that will give women equal pay and a bit more power.

Sheila: Look, the unions have had an Equal Pay for women thing down on the TUC statute books since 1889, and they've done nothing. This Act isn't going to make any difference.

Annie: Of course it's going to be evaded, and it will be quite hard work to get it enforced, but you can't avoid the things women have to fight for at work, you can't pull women out of work, out of the unions, just because housework isn't recognised by a direct wage.

Sheila: Women need money of their own. We don't want any more housekeeping dollops. We want our own money for the housework we do. Just think what would happen if every single woman went on strike, refused to do housework.

Susan: What a fantastic idea.

Annie: A very nice symbolic action, but on its own it gets us exactly nowhere. You're just arguing women into complete inactivity, not more and better activity.

Sheila: You're so bloody superior, Annie, you and your nice little middle-class husband, nice little part-time jobs, you just condescend to women who are on the breadline, fucked over by their husbands, exploited by the capitalists. . .

Annie (very very calm): Rachel has a part-time job.

Sheila: And her guy does fuck-all.

Rachel: He works a ten-hour day, Sheil. You know that. He's away half the time. That's not his choice. That's his job.

Sheila: Women's power isn't going to come from the unions, it's going to come from being organised as women. That's when the class will be strong.

Ruth: What class?

Sheila: The working class.

Ruth: But women aren't a class, Sheila.

To and fro, weaving, sometimes tied back to the point, moving from point to point, guided by Jennifer, each woman deeply involved with the dual effort of formulating an opinion and arguing for it at the same time. The argument often taking the form of assertion pitted against assertion, women trained for so long to hide their intelligence, to be polite, show an interest in other people, draw them out with questions, now in the relative security burst out with a pent-up aggression, asserting themselves, their opinions. A testing ground with other women in which the moments of assertion were not always secure, in which women attacked and were attacked, in which in an inverted way we both used the consciousness-raising groups to assert a new independence, a new self-determination, and at the same time to express the unarticulated tensions we felt in the other areas of our lives. Often the tensions made it appear as though there was a ring of invisible men sitting outside the circle of women, a silent audience whose approval we often still needed.

Annie had been slotting in and out of the discussion, focussing as much on Sheila as on her desire to make a logical sense out of the argument. She felt exhausted; she had not spoken for ten minutes and felt that unless she said something soon she would disappear. The network of warm nuances, security, so important to the weekly meeting, the 'sisterhood' of which they all so proudly spoke outside the group, was no longer the fine-spun filigree in which air and light and communication were held. The filaments were now electrified, buzzed when touched, couldn't avoid being touched, everyone was so close.

Jennifer: Ruth, what you were saying earlier, about women and class, could we go back to that, could you develop that a bit?

Ruth: Well, this business about housework being unwaged. I don't think that's right. I mean, wages, benefits from the welfare state — the cost of reproducing labour power, which is really what the wages for housework argument turns on, this cost is covered in a variety of ways — not adequately, that's true and working class women are most vulnerable, but I don't think we can say simply that housework, childcare is given free, is not paid for at all.

Sheila: But women must have money of our own.

Ruth: I agree. But calling it wages for housework not only simplifies the solution, it also simplifies the problem. But I'm not very clear. I must read the pamphlet again.

The filigree flashed. Annie thought, Ruthie, you liar, you do know, you're just holding back in case we think you're being heavy, theoretical *male* for godsake. Male. What's male about using your head. Nothing intrinsic and you bloody know it. Games feminists play. 'I'm not very clear' my arse.

Annie: Sheila, it strikes me that one of the main problems with the argument is just what Ruth said: wages for housework is a kind of global undefined demand which sucks everything into it like a whirlpool, and ignores all the other demands — what about equal pay, what about equal educational opportunities, what about contraception and abortion, what about nurseries — there's no short-term strategy in it, let alone long-term strategy. What about the rest of women's experiences, the rest of working class experience?

Sheila: You're just sloganising.

Susan: Yes, the pamphlet doesn't ignore those other things.

Annie: But it says wages for housework is the centre, the uniting demand and that's just wrong.

Sheila: You're so bloody smug, aren't you? What do you know about the working class?

Rachel: Watch out, there's a spy about.

Sheila: Well, I think it's a bit unnecessary to put me on the spot — this isn't a bloody inquisition. It's so bloody personal.

Annie: Sheila, it's not personal, we are actually having a political disagreement, in case you hadn't noticed.

The meeting that evening went on late, till eleven.

Annie walked to the bus stop with Ruth and Jennifer, Sheila went off on her bike and Rachel walked home. None of them talked much, but Ruth tentatively suggested as a parting thought that perhaps they should think about doing some more systematic theoretical study.

Sheila and Annie did not contact each other during the following week: Annie planned to invite Sheila back for coffee after the next meeting, to have a friendly talk, away from the hothouse of the group, but Sheila sent her apologies to the meeting. Annie veered between an irritated disappointment and a suspicion that perhaps Sheila was avoiding her.

The group did not have another discussion about wages for housework as such, although they did for some months follow Ruth's prepared reading list — an introductory series of Marxist texts, and the issue of wages for housework emerged again through that, in a theoretical discussion. In the meantime the women's liberation movement was changing rapidly; expanding, feminists were becoming active in a whole range of trade union activities, setting up women's centres, refuges for battered wives, all kinds of research, discussion. . . the group, although it continued to meet, give or take a member or two, for a further four years, was a friendship, a support group of women who had struggled through to political consciousness together, and whose own political allegiances sparked off in many directions: a gay commune, further teaching, trade union organising, membership of one of the numerous revolutionary left-wing groupings which flourished in the seventies, involved in producing feminist journals. What they each gained separately was a greater individual confidence and capacity for self-determination as women, and each of them fed that confidence back into a variety of struggles to change the position of women, and in the case of the majority of women in that particular group, to a struggle for some kind of socialism.

So in their ways did Sheila and Annie. Sheila committed herself completely to working with the group that campaigned for wages for housework. Annie watched her group's progress with interest; the literature they produced and the meetings they held had a certain sort of agente provocateuse element in them. None of the arguments, she thought, held up to any serious analysis; at best they provoked people into thought about housework, at worst they antagonised large numbers of women and hostility in all men and women who worked in the labour movement in any way. At least, that much Annie gathered from other discussions and the political writing which flourished at the time.

Sheila only came to two more group meetings. Annie missed the first, she had flu; every time Annie felt an urge to phone Sheila something held her back — a kind of fearful pride. Fearing a more violent explosion of disagreement, pride in not wanting to be the first to make a move. It was not something she was ever able to discuss thoroughly with Mike.

The second and last time Sheila came back to the group was some months later. There were two new women who had joined the group to take part in the study programme. Sheila burst in late, breathless from a hilarious encounter between a raw young policeman and a group of women night cleaners picketing a building from which two of them had been sacked. The women had made great play with brooms and buckets, sweeping the pavement around the policeman's feet till he was forced to jump over them to avoid being floored. Next time round on his beat he made sure he crossed the road.

As Sheila told the story, everyone joined in her laughter, as though they too were remembering a shared experience, Annie too. But after the laughter died down, her eyes met Sheila's and they both quickly looked away. The political shades were down.

(*Editorial note*: some of the words and phrases used in this piece will be explained in the course of our historical series on feminism: eg, consciousness-raising, gay, Vietnam war, student politics, housewife.)

Parallel Lines
Sara Maitland

1. Dear Carole,
In the first place am I allowed to say I'm surprised to find you working for *Liberation Time*; isn't it just a little glossy for you? On the other hand if you're there perhaps it isn't that bad. Anyway I'm glad it's you because I feel freer to say a couple of things.

Firstly, if you think you're going to get a feminist 'martyr's' story out of this mess you'll simply make fools of yourselves. Ten days for contempt is hardly spectacular in itself, and the form that our 'protest' took can hardly be called noble. Kathy screaming and fainting, although emotionally legitimate, is hardly the image of the strong woman, and Joan and I yelling abuse and throwing ink at the Clerk will appear irresponsible and silly if presented outside of what it was all about. Not wanting to be presented as silly in your magazine, or anywhere else, I really do think you should play down the heroism angle.

Secondly, do I catch just a hint in your letter that you want to make some 'working class feminist' copy out of this? Because it won't work; you can present Kathy like that, but if you know Joan at all you'll know that is a wash out. As for me, my antecedents may be OK but you, if anyone, know that I sold my working-class heritage right down the river the very first evening I walked into that dining room at college and conceived a deep envy of most of the women there, including you; not a bitter envy, an admiring one.

However, you say you want to run a piece on the three of us: 'something personalised, but not of course a-political' — come on Carole, love, wake up — and so 'why don't we write and tell you how we came to join the women's movement'.

I'm writing this from inside (secretly you know I can't help feeling just a little proud being able to write that) though presumably I won't be able to post it till after I get out; but it means I haven't had a chance to get together with Joan and Kathy so I don't know what their response will be, but I can guess. Kathy won't answer at all: she has now been moved to the prison hospital unit as 'hysterical and unmanageable' and next week will doubtless be transferred to a handy mental hospital. Joan on the other hand will have given you a brief doctrinal essay on class analysis and the nuclear family structures. They are both right of course, but feeling lonely and isolated I shall indulge myself and tell you how I came to join the women's movement. I don't know if it's what you had in mind, but here it is.

Throughout my childhood I hated my parents, was embarrassed by them all the time. Not for the reason that middle-class lefties usually offer, but for the opposite reason: they were heavily committed left-wingers. Both of them. Minor Union Officials at their separate places of work, activists, meeting holders. My mother even went to the unforgiveable lengths of supporting immigrants and getting them welfare rights. She didn't keep the house clean, she didn't dress nicely and she went out to work with enthusiasm. You can imagine my humiliation. Everyone on our estate knew them and criticised them. When we did the Industrial Revolution in school the teacher said, not absolutely kindly, 'I'm sure Sheila can tell us about the Rise of the Labour Movement.' Worse still, I could. And no-one ever asked me for a date.

Well, I don't know if you know but every September there is this fair in Oxford, the St Giles' Fair. The whole of the centre of town is blocked off for it. It's a real fair, what they are meant to be like you know, both sleazy and romantic. The year I was fourteen Jonathon Carter asked me to go to the fair with him. Wow. You can't imagine. Jonathon Carter. He was a year above me in school, good looking, good at work, good at everything. The school stud. And he came from one of those big North Oxford Houses; I think his father was actually a teacher in the University. Status that's what Jon Carter was. 'I'm going to the Fair with Jon Carter.' '*You* are? With Jon-a-thon Carter?' It was my big romance. It took me the whole week to decide what to wear. I insisted on going up town alone on the bus so he wouldn't have to see where I lived. I spent my meagre savings on more make-up. Every feminine wile known to a fourteen-year-old I employed. I built that date up into the biggest deal since the War.

We had a wonderful evening. When the ferris wheel stopped at the very top he kissed me, swaying up there among the trees and the lights, and when he groped around my thighs I wished I hadn't worn tights. And then we walked about holding hands and I felt so good. And we rode on the Victorian Merry-go-round which must be one of the great romantic experiences of the western world and he grinned at me all lop-sided and *I was in love*. And we shared a candy floss and wished there was somewhere we could go together. And just as it started to get late we stopped briefly in front of one of those shooting stands where you have to knock down a little moving duck with an air-rifle. On the stall there was

this stupid stuffed monkey as a prize and I said, 'Look isn't that sweet.'
And Jon Carter gave this big manly grin at my sweet little ways and said,
'Shall I try and win it for you?' So he paid his money and loaded his
shots, and made a great fuss about taking up a position, leaning forward
and backwards and taking hours to aim, and missed five times. He looked
a bit put out and said in this knowledgeable way which impressed me,
'They always cook the guns you know, bend the barrels or shift the sights
a little,' and laughed self-consciously. And I said, 'O, can I have a go?'
And Jon and the stallkeeper exchanged this little masculine-conspiracy
grin, and he indulgently shelled out the necessary shilling or whatever it
was, and picked up the gun and loaded it for me, kindly indicating where
the trigger was. So I put my elbows on the stall, looked at the little duck
and fired, the little duck fell over promptly. Jon said, 'Good shot' and
laughed, but he let me load the next shot for myself. I don't know what
came over me, afterwards I knew quite well I should have missed after
that one faintly amusing fluke, but I just wanted to impress him as he
impressed me, and I shot that stupid duck five times in a row, with my
elbows not moving from the stall, and not even looking around for
applause. The man in charge laughed and handed over my monkey and
grinned at Jon and told him not to bring me any more as he couldn't
afford it, and I giggled and looked up at Jon.

And suddenly I realised what I had done. His face was blank, hurt and
furious all at once. 'Beginners Luck,' I almost shouted, desperate, and
then when his expression did not change I even told him the shameful
truth, 'I'm sorry, my grandad taught me, he's a gamekeeper.'

It did no good; his fury and my shame increased by the moment.
Within minutes I was almost in tears. I was broken by shame, sickened by
the hurt I'd inflicted on him just to show-off. After less than five minutes
I said I would have to go and catch my bus. We walked to the bus stop. I
said, 'Thank you for a smashing time. You don't have to wait.' And he
didn't; he pecked me on the cheek and walked off. At least I was free to
cry. I threw that bloody monkey down in the street and sobbed and
sobbed and sobbed. I groped my way onto the Number One bus and
wept all the way home. What I had always been afraid of was proved true:
I was not a real woman and I never would be.

After a whole week of shame and misery I told my Mum about it.
She'd had a fight with my Dad which made it easier somehow, at least I
knew she wouldn't tell him. She listened to my garbled account and then
said, 'Damn men. You've had a bloody miserable week because he can't
shoot straight. That's the way it is.' Then she laughed, 'I bet when they
go on the street they'll keep people like you at home so the enemy won't
find out you can shoot straighter than they can.' But she wasn't laughing
at me.

And after that it was just a question of waiting until there was a women's movement to join. A simplification of course, there were lots more things and reasons. But that was the moment of recognition that I had been ripped off, not as a child or as a working class person — though that probably comes into it too — but as a woman. And it bloody well wasn't fair.

You can do what you like with this little saga. I'll be in Oxford for a week when I get out of here and you can't get in touch with me there because we're not on the phone, but I'll be back in the House by the 18th. Why don't you come and see us all there? I don't think you should write the article anyway until you've seen the commune.

While on the subject of the article; do please be careful how you put anything about Kathy having cracked up; it will be difficult to cite her natural distress as a mother without implying she is incompetent as a person (which she isn't) — I mean of course to anyone who is looking for some justification for the court's decision to take her kids. This is important: even the court never cited nervous disability or personal incompetence, only her life style and her relationship with Joan. Which reminds me, I'm writing pretty freely because of knowing you and because of being bored here but you're not to follow *any* of this up unless you get the go ahead from Joan, because she's so much more personally implicated, and because she should have a stronger sense of what Kathy would feel. What seems difficult for me right now and probably why I relapsed into the personally nostalgic, is that although we've managed to get a lot of publicity about the really masculist ways custody courts work and have probably made a hell of a lot of ignorant people realise what is going on, nonetheless we've probably totally ruined any chance *Kathy* herself ever had of getting the custody of her own kids away from her crazy parents. That's where your martyrdom bit comes in. Nice being in touch with you again anyway,

see you, love Sheila.

2. Dear *Liberation Time*,

Thank you for your letter and apologies I didn't get round to answering it before. I didn't find the accommodation provided for me by Her Majesty's Government conducive to analysis. Sheila says she did write to you from inside, but was worried that what she'd written might seem like 'garbled sentiment'. But she probably said that because she thought I would think it 'garbled sentiment'. I haven't seen Kathy yet; she's been removed to the Walton Clinic and they repeat ad nauseam that she's not yet up to receiving visitors. There ought to be some way of breaking through, and we've contacted Margaret Matthews, her solicitor. Perhaps you can help us here, shove it in your article at least. We can't even find out if she's been sectioned or if she's gone 'voluntarily', though I can't see that it will make much difference. For obvious reasons it may not actually help for me to be militant about seeing her. Sheila and Beth are working on it.

How I joined the Women's Movement? In personalised terms. I thought we were fighting the cult of the personality, but then you do have to get an article together. I can't write and tell you how I was slaving over a hot stove stirring my husband's dinner when suddenly I recognised the terms of my oppression. It was never like that. I joined the Women's Movement, in as much as you can 'join' it, by leaving IS. I joined the Women's Movement specifically, when I realised that women relate to the modes of production differently from all the other groups of equally exploited workers, and that moreover most men in the left didn't want to know about it, or give a shit. Once those facts are granted, and I do realise that they are not universally granted yet, obviously it is not enough to engage in the proletarian revolution only. This is not presented as a novel or exciting analysis, it is simply the reason why I joined the Women's Movement.

I do realise that this is probably not what you want, but I believe it is important to see this whole business of Kathy and her kids as a political not a sentimental cause. How can I explain this, when as was dragged up at the hearing, I have been living with Kathy for eleven months, when it was finally the fact of my sexual relationship with her that must have decided the court. Because looked at even in *their* terms it was an extraordinary decision: they gave the girls' care into the hands of an elderly, and on the clearest evidence neurotic couple who had already — in the terms of the state — made a mess of bringing up their own daughter, rather than let the children remain with their mother — even though their father was not willing to contest this very actively himself. Even the judge said that Kathy had reasonable grounds for seeking the dissolution of her marriage. It was a political case: her politically avowed sexuality and her open radical views. It was Kathy's decision, although not her decision alone, to fight this case as a political statement about the structures of the family. She could have put on a nice skirt and said she would have no more to do with that sinister lefty commune and its immoralities. Kathy is not a victim of our political enthusiasms, but of the state's denial of personal lives for women. One problem with Kathy's breakdown is that it will make it only too easy for them to present her as a simple working-girl dominated by middle-class intellectual lefties; and all else aside this is such a bloody insult to one of the real fighters inside the Women's Movement. The funny thing is that if the commune had kidnapped her kids or something, her breakdown would be seen as touching proof of the strength of her wonderful profound maternal feelings. But when they do the kidnapping it becomes proof of her inadequacy.

I don't expect this is what you wanted, but I don't feel now is the time for the agonies of oppression in a professional class, Catholic family. Sometime in the future though you might do something on Women's Prisons; and I'll give you the True Confessions bit then if you like.

Yours, Joan Westbury

P.S. Sheila and I want to see what you're planning to run before it goes to print. OK?

3. Dear Carole Mercier,
Thank you for writing to me from your magazine. I'm sorry I haven't answered before, but it's not easy here, although better since Margaret, that's my solicitor, has been. They won't let me see any of the women from the house as they say it will upset me.

Also you can see my handwriting is a bit wobbly, which I put down to the drugs — I feel wrapped in cotton wool. They have you in a neat trap here: if you take your medicines you are slow and can't fight; if you don't take them, they can use it as a proof that you need them and then they are free to force you.

Thank you for your letter, it does make a difference, I haven't seen anyone and I don't know what is going on. You want to know why I'm in the women's movement? Please only use this letter if Joan and Sheila say that's OK because they know what the scene is, and I haven't seen anyone so I don't know what's happening, but I will try and tell you.

Most of the reasons came up in court I think. I was married when I was seventeen, mostly to get away from home; and I stayed married for eight bloody years, I didn't know what to do, and I couldn't get out. I had the girls which was good anyway, but Joe beat me up most of the time, from the start really, and after I had the miscarriage when he pushed me down the stairs I gave up and left. I had nowhere to go, because my parents wouldn't have me back because they don't believe in divorce and at the time said they couldn't cope with the kids. No one believes that now, they just threw me out when I had nowhere to go. They don't want the girls, they just hate me. Look, I'm sorry, this all sounds crazy; I know the doctor here thinks I'm crazy, all he ever talks about is being gay, but when I try to tell him about Joe or my parents you can feel him switch off, he thinks I'm crazy. Anyway in the end I went to the Women's Aid Refuge and everything changed; so after a while I went to live in the House and really joined the Movement, and everything began to make sense. I know I got hysterical in the court, and I hope I didn't let anyone down too badly, but for the first time in my life the girls and I were happy and having something that could be called a life together. And they were going to take it away from us. For the first time in my life I didn't feel a fool all the time, I didn't have to feel embarrassed, above all I didn't feel frightened stupid all the time. That is what they were taking away from me. When I said in court I would rather Joe had the children than my parents did I really meant it, at least he has some right to them and never hurt them, I think in his own sick way he did love them, while my parents can't love anyone. They're sick. They're tight, hating people, who use their horrible religion as a way of putting everybody else down. The court seems to think that they'll get 'decent advantages' living with them; frilly dresses for Sunday School where they can learn that God hates women. They are so unfit to look after children. I'm worried out of my mind about what will happen to the girls. Julie is old enough to be miserable with them, and Marie will grow up hating me and everything I wanted them to have. I'm sorry to go on like this, but I haven't seen anyone, I haven't got anyone to talk to and I have to make up my mind. It's terribly difficult. If I play their game I reckon I could get out of here before too long, and then in a year or so I could have another go at getting the girls back, but that would mean giving everything up, the House and Joan and all my friends and living a completely straight life for at least ten years. I think this might be better for the kids, but then what about me? Without the Women's Movement and the House and everything I don't think I could keep it together anyway. And then there's me and my own life; I worry if I gave it up for them I might come to hate my girls, they might as well be hated by my parents with some of the things of life as by me on SS. And another thing is I just want to have them back. Even if they were happy and OK and everything I still want them back. I miss them and want them all the time. Sometimes I feel I would do anything to get them back.

I am sorry to go on and on like this, but I really am frightened and worried, especially as I don't know what's going on. If you write the article please be careful that none of the blame falls on Joan and especially not on Sheila. Joan is not as tough as she likes to think (and don't show her this letter) and Sheila got involved out of sisterhood, it never need have been her problem. She would say this was not the point and of course she's right, but I would hate to think she'd got messed up or lost her job because of us. Margaret said they had both said they would go to Court and say they had bullied and intimidated me if this would help to get the kids back, and although sometimes when I think of the girls I think I'd do anything to get them back, I won't do that, because it isn't true and would make a waste of everything we've tried to say.

I'm sorry going on and on, but apart from when Margaret came last week I haven't seen anyone and I don't want to write to Joan or to the House in case they use it to keep me here longer.

Thank you for writing, it is good to hear that people are on our side; the side of women who want just to live the way they want to and get those bastards off our backs.

in sisterhood, Kathy Spencer

P.S. If you could get a message to Joan tell her lots of love and to Sheila and the others too. I'm working on being back with them. Sisterhood is powerful.

THREE

Feminist fiction and aesthetics

We are happy to throw the word feminist around enough to make our didactic purpose clear: along with feminists in other fields we are convinced that the bias in favour of male-dominance in this society not only distorts the true state of affairs but cripples the development of the whole.

But there is something else that in the act of working on and presenting short stories we are saying. These political ideas, about which all of us could (and indeed have) written in non 'art' media, can and may be formed into those patterns which people generally agree to call Art. *And* this is a worthwhile activity.

This is not a dogmatic credo: it is our experience of having spent eighteen months doing it (you can call it self-justification if you like but you'll be wrong). We are saying, having written and read, that these fictions have a life and function different (not better or worse) from the same ideas presented through other media. This difference works in two directions: different for the producer and different for the consumer, the writer and the reader. Art forms render ideas accessible to readers who could not receive those insights in any other format. Art permits types of expression to some writers which could not be manifested by them in any other way. (This is more obviously true with the plastic or aural arts, but is also true of writing.) We could, and people have, written articles or books or pamphlets or essays on the Feminist Interpretation of History, or The Involvement and Role of Men Within the Women's Movement, without making these ideas palatable to people who may like *Penelope* or *Time, Gentlemen*, and without liberating legitimate emotional and intellectual desires within ourselves.

Some of this problem of accessibility is caused by cultural conditioning. Speaking for myself, for example, I find it much easier to read fiction, probably because my father had very little interest in abstract theory and taught me to see ideas through practical action (history, fiction, applied mechanics). But it is also related to the nature of art itself. Art is an artificial organisation of experience; the most 'realistic' art is totally selective, it cannot be random, without specific (if hidden) viewpoint. Its aim — usually well hidden — is to create a microcosm sufficiently satisfying for the reader to want to consent to it. To go beyond a 'willing suspension of disbelief' and convince or beguile the reader into agreeing that this is how things are (or were or could be). Not necessarily in any intellectual sense, but in the emotional sense of this corresponds to and makes meaning of my personal experience.

In this light it is fair to describe all art as political. It is important to recognise, in individual artefacts, the political content; to examine them with an eye to discovering what the disguised viewpoint of the artist was. In part it is because we wish to reassert this fact that we have arranged this book in this way. In the first section we photograph our experience (the camera does not point randomly, we choose what we see through the lens) and present a picture of ourselves as women engagées — against social convention, economic and sexual exploitation, our own social conditioning. Then we subject that picture to a political examination: the analysis of the Women's Movement politics, sexuality, psychology, group dynamics, intellectual issues.

And now in the last section we can claim that our art is no longer, thanks to the political filter through which we have dragged it (and ourselves, and you), a private presentation of our individual experience. It is no longer a cry of anguish or a whimper at the disagreeableness of things in general and men in particular. It is becoming a struggle to express, render accessible and dynamic our interpretation, not of our experience alone, but of experience at large. Not only as it is but as it might be.

Now we can say: men are involved in this — *Time, Gentlemen*. All women, whether they know or care are involved in these contradictions — *Radio Times* and *You Only Have to Say*. Our whole history and the structures of consolation (myths) that we have built for ourselves need to be and can be transformed — *Penelope*. And at this historical point there are divisions and alienations we cannot even offer solutions to — *After-life*.

We are saying something else too, about the way we look at art. Much of our training as readers or critics seems to be aimed at facilitating us to make judgements of the 'good, better, best' type. To build hierarchies of merit (the best authors, the best works of the best authors etc). Some of this is inevitable — my four-year-old already likes some books better than others — but within the context of this book value judgements of this sort between writer and writer are divisive. They are an easy habit, a simplifying way to read this; but they will distort our intentions and hide what we are doing. This is not an anthology, it is a book, a single entity, an accumulation of points of view.

There are fifteen stories in this book. I think they are interesting stories, all of them, by any canon of taste. Most of them were written without reference to the schema by which we are presenting them, some of them were slotted into their sections by brute force. But this arrangement is neither casual nor arbitrary: it consciously reflects some facts about art, which are often, in our culture, hidden or denied.

Art is a way of organising experience in order to clarify it. In this case, not one private experience, but a diverse collective experience. To arrange these stories on an intellectual, considered basis (rather than by author, by alphabetical order of title, or something similar) not only reflects this fact as clearly as possible it also demands that you consider it.

Art is artificial and polemical. This applies not only to the stories individually, but to their presentation as one book, a single artefact. In presenting these stories in an obviously artificial and explicitly polemical way (and then writing little notes to make sure you get the point) we are stating that we are not ashamed of this inevitable function of art. We are conscious of it and prepared to use it for our own ends, and then to let on that we are doing so.

Art and the artist have been mystified, reified and isolated in our society. We are trying to talk about method, and process and collectivity. If this fact and our open didacticism make it more difficult for you to read these stories as 'art' in any traditional ivory-tower sense of the word, so much the better.

Sara Maitland

Afterlife
Valerie Miner

'I've got to get back to work.'

'Ellen will be hurt if you go.'

'Ridiculous. With twenty other people here, she doesn't have to talk with me. Besides, she's tucked in the corner with that Englishman.'

'Then there's Hank. Remember how hard it was to approach an instructor when you were in art school?'

'Fuck Hank. I've had enough playing luminary. I've got my own work to do.'

Trying to stop bickering with herself, Carol turned and inspected the Guatemalan tapestry on the floor next to her. Ellen did have good taste. Of course it was more than friendship that placed her sculpture on the corner of Ellen's mantlepiece. Carol wished Hank would hurry the hell up with that cheese and wine. She hoped he would remember 'dry'; she couldn't handle a hangover tomorrow. She had too much work to do. What to do while she waited? Thirty years old and still worrying whether she should skim the album covers or the book jackets. Really, she had better things to spend her time on. She had to finish that park sculpture. It had become an obsession. Her friends had learned to treat it like a difficult child — or treat her like a difficult parent — inquiring tentatively, offering generous, but puzzled sympathy.

Carol left the party quickly, not bothering to disturb Ellen from the Englishman or Hank from the gobs of sweaty cheese. They would understand.

('An artist, you know, actually makes her living by it. Maybe a little shy, eccentric, maybe even a little neurotic about her work, but in a productive way.')

She often left in the middle of an evening to go back to the studio — as if she had never been graded for deportment in primary school. Such a waste of time, these civil banalities, anecdotes, pick-ups. She was dismayed to find herself getting slightly fatter and slightly duller and slightly older. Lately, it was easier to look downhill — only three more days until Friday; only two more hours until bed. Parties and leisurely lunches and midnight telephone conversations all seemed so extraneous, *such a waste of time*. They interrupted work and postponed sleep. How she had spent so many hours just lying around listening to her clock radio when she was fourteen or talking to Guy in their tiny kitchen when they were first married. There just seemed to be more time then.

The street lamps along Shattuck Avenue condensed the cold night into stalactites of potential energy. The cars cut through the luminous fog, sliding across the bridge to San Francisco. San Francisco. Her father had worked in all those greasy aircraft factories to be stationed someday in San Francisco. San Francisco was why she moved school after school, why the family wound up in a Lockeed suburb of Palo Alto. San Francisco of Oriental steamers, gold rushes, Spanish padres, earthquakes, home.

(Nightmares still. Coming back from class and finding the empty house in Trenton or Cleveland or Seattle. Searching for the family on the road to San Francisco. Finding them in the hall of mirrors, endless, beginningless mirrors at Palisades Park.)

She often saw herself in San Francisco. Having a retrospective at the Palace of Fine Arts, teaching at the Institute, working in a studio overlooking the Golden Gate. But she was still in Berkeley, taking the Number 51 bus to her studio on the Northside of the Cal campus. She had a good view of the City from her back window when the eucalyptus wasn't in bloom.

She climbed Hearst and looked down at the cold stillness. They told her she shouldn't walk at night, but they didn't know what they were talking about. They said they were afraid of muggers, but she knew they were afraid of the stillness. Nothing but clear winter and the City across the water. Winter — a survival course of contemplation and work — enlarged her. She cherished the grey, the constant steel grey. San Francisco grey. She had read Thomas Wolfe and had gone to Britain, but the London fog — even the Fife haar — was shadowy rather than grey.

Carol was finally accepting that there was something intrinsically *wrong* with the park sculpture. Sometimes you had to destroy to create, right? It takes guts to admit you've failed. The piece was too cognitive. It said what she *thought*, but had no *emotional* integrity. She would probably have to begin all over again.

Carol was good at beginnings. 'Engagé', as her mother's friend who read Lillian Hellman would say. Everyone envied Carol's drive and energy. Everyone knew she would *make it* one day, because she knew what she wanted. By the time she was twenty-six, she had broken through the traditions of the Bay Area galleries. Just about at the top. And yet everyone still respected her. While her friends opted out for money or prestige or marriage, Carol had — as Ellen admiringly put it — 'sanitized herself of sexist, capitalist compromises'. She was free of motherhood, wifery, careerism. She was free. That's the way they saw it. Free to get on with it.

She let the empty night buses trundle past her. Tonight she couldn't be encapsuled. That was why she left the party. It hadn't been any more boring than most. The music had been good. And she had actually fancied that Englishman. She couldn't tolerate the warm, smokey room. She couldn't play lady. Ellen hadn't done anything except sit, but it was the *way* she sat. Just as it was the *way* she spoke (for surely Carol and Ellen agreed on all the issues). They just had different ways. In the end, although Carol knew the Englishman preferred her, she let Ellen have her way. And she went on hers.

('No, Guy, it's nothing you've done. I just can't continue to be Professor Thompson's wife. Not your *fault*. Not anyone's *fault*.')

Arthritis in her left leg, divorced, childless, poor. She made the abstract rebuttals: talented, accomplished, self-sufficient, brave. She had the argument often lately; she just wasn't concentrating on her work. She had to stop procrastinating. It had been due three weeks ago. Clearly, she should have finished it last month. But she had been paralysed. She had always met deadlines, but lately she regressed into this childhood where she refused to work, where she waited for someone to motivate her, challenge her, cajole, scold. The punishment was something she could manage for herself, guilt being an ubiquitous noose.

She pushed open the door and switched on the light. She felt the cold immediately, realising that she had been walking all the way with her coat open. She enjoyed working here. She could have got a studio at the college but she liked to keep the parts of her life distinct. She worked here in the afternoons and early evenings. At night, in the apartment upstairs, she used to have friends round for coffee or for meetings of the party or the rape crisis group. But she hadn't invited anyone since January. She had started sleeping at the studio. She had to get the sculpture done. She thought that by spending so much time with it . . . covered in an old sheet, like empty words shrouding silence . . . that by living with it. Well, she just couldn't give up an important commission like that. Carol plugged in the electric fire, turned on the kettle and dismissed her mother's warnings about conflagration as she made her way upstairs to the bathroom.

The heat still hadn't stretched across the room by the time she returned, so she stood and warmed her hands on the cracking green elephant mug. She should throw it away. Cracks cultivated germs. Besides, someday the thing would split in her hands. It was a kind of trophy. Professor Ash's mug. Her work had such control, he said. She was a good student, but he didn't want to give her any false hopes. Most girls chose a practical programme like teaching or design.

She stared at the block of stone which hulked in the middle of the long empty room like a Lenten statue. What was she waiting for? She pulled away the cloth and saw the same thing she had left that afternoon. The foundation was right — the heavy chunks on bare blocks. Heavy but not clumsy. Clean, but not cold. She didn't know what, but something was utterly wrong.

She turned from it again, opened the window for some fresh air and looked across the Bay. She couldn't see through the fog to the City skyline. The low cloud ceiling suspended Berkeley in light night, as though under a private moon. Next to the window was her own resin relief of a window — glossy green and orange irony. And next to that, a stream of magicians' scarves she had brought back from India. She liked the room: the shelf of Victorian novels, the postcards of workers she had picked up at the galleries. She felt reassured, as natural as one might feel in a personal shrine.

She moved her hands along the curves she had smoothed last week. The large circle in the middle was particularly comfortable. *Not* a womb, she anticipated Karl's criticism: schizophrenic — the hard masculinity of the base vs. the voluptuous trunk. Still if it wasn't bloody transsexual as Karl would say or a dialectic, as Miriam would say, it *was* unfinished. She needed a head, a top, an end, no, a beginning. What was she trying to do with it? She had reached this point three weeks ago. She had begun to feel desperate, crazy. She had tried everything.

A change of scene. Reality therapy. She had gone to the proposed site of the sculpture in the south end of the park. Golden Gate Park in the mist of March, cold and deserted, except for a few dossers biding time between hours at the mission. And a mother with her little blonde daughter in a red coat. Familiar sensation, but no memory of her's surely. The only walks she ever took with her mother were around shopping centres. Once there had been a television programme — she must have been eight or nine — of a family hiking through dry birch leaves. And she remembered vowing then that she would take her children for walks in the park. Blond children. She had married Guy for blond children.

(She woke up asking how long it would take.
'Don't worry, Mrs Thompson. It's a simple procedure.'
'No muss. No fuss.'
'We'll have it removed in twenty minutes. Good job you didn't wait

much longer.'
'I can't now. Someday. But now there's too much work. Ten.'
'That's it. Backwards with me now. Nine-Eight-Seven. . . .'
'Rustling leaves — crackling like fresh ham — rustling.'
'That's it dear, think pleasant thoughts. That's natural.'
'I am a natural woman.'
'Don't try to talk now, dear. Think about the little girl rustling.'
'Little girl, how can you tell?'
'About\yourself as a little girl, rustling. . .'
Rustling like the taffeta of nuns' slips. Nuns don't have children
either. But everyone is their child. We are all God's children.
Thou shalt not kill.
'A simple procedure.'
Extreme unction by nitrous oxide.
'Carol, it was an operation after all. You're supposed to be resting.
Put down the sketch pad for a while. You can't go straight back to
work.'
'A simple procedure.'

A blank, that day in the park. She returned to the same place, without
a head. She felt bloody impotent. They called it bronchitis, an impossible
love affair, severe depression. But she knew: her will had *run down*.
Maybe she could do the sculpture from a fresh piece. She had thrown away
parts of her life before. Yes, she would begin again from a completely
new block.
KKKK buzzed surrender to Saturday night. 2.30. How long had she
been phased out, oblivious to this seething sound. She had done this so
often lately, lost concentration, consciousness. She would find herself
frozen for minutes, asleep, numb, paralysed. Euthanasia should be
legalised for those without brainwaves. She swished the dial for company,
for the speedy-dosey monologues of adolescent dj's who giggle to
themselves in the night.

('Ms Thompson, the partners have discussed it and much as we respect
your diligence, much as we acknowledge your talent, we do not find
your work acceptable. It's a matter of, well, taking directions. Any
design firm depends on cooperation. Perhaps we were wrong to try out
a woman in this rather, uh, comradely ambience. And perhaps you
are, ultimately, an individualist. Perhaps you should do some sort of
freelance work. It's a question of personality, really. Perhaps after
you've tried your wings, we could consider continuing.')

Carol welcomed the electronic scapeghosts. Inane pop music — healthy
outlet for anger. It was either them or her. Or her work. After all that

struggling — passionate as it was in feminist terms — what did she have? A parable for her friends' daughters. A reputation? What was that but a mortgage on future work.

The time she wasn't sculpting, she should have been sculpting. Borrowed hollows of time. When she couldn't sculpt, she couldn't teach and she couldn't party. The integrated contemporary woman, disintegrated. Suffocated by other people's respect. Tired, chilled and alone in a draughty old garage with an expensive hulk of rock. She examined the incomplete lines with the close cruelty of a middle aged woman counting her wrinkles in the mirror. Maybe she should go back to the reliefs. Jube Jube resin and scrap brass. They sold well, brought decent reviews, provided a comfortable competence. Mediocre, perhaps, but she didn't feel like an imposter.

No. *No.* She just wasn't concentrating. She switched off the radio and lifted the top of her stereo, irritated to find she had forgotten to put two records back. She set them over the turntable and pressed the reject button. Marya Terazinya haunted her. It was Carol's own fault. She had sought out the woman after that night of San Saens at the Albert Hall. Carol hunted all over London for the faint Soviet recording of Marya's concerti. She found herself leafing through music journals on Charing Cross Road, trying to learn more about the pianist. Young and ascetic. No time for anything but her music. She lived in a Moscow bedsit with her piano. A spare life, but like Sister Matthew, she knew there was another one. The concerto ended with a wrench of the armature, a plastic pop of the next record and a loud, brassy voice.

'Bill Bailey, Wontya . . . ' How Carole *hated* that song. A pre-feminist objection. Recalling *another* Ed Sullivan Sunday night. . . and the fat, blonde woman in the sequined gown bellowing for forgiveness. . . 'A really big hand for Sandy Samone.' Carol remembered her mother leaning heavier on the iron, looking from the flickering screen to her husband, 'Right, Merv. I'll pay the rent when we get a place. Just you get us to San Francisco.'

(She should have gone home an hour ago, but Carol was fascinated by the woman at the piano bar at Dennyman's. She had come all the way out to Hayward to see her. Older now. Blonder. But the same voice, the same mellow mediocrity, despite this sixth vodka and orange — 'An admirer,' Carol had asked the barman to say — and the lady continued to sing.

Sandy Samone didn't know that ten thousand miles away in a yesterday that was still today in the objectivity of international time treaties, Marya Terazinya was dead. A heart attack, according to Pravda. No further details . . . only time crosses borders easily. Would that it were

so easy to cross time. Of course Sandy Samone wouldn't know Marya
Terazinya. Not to be elitist, but it was the difference between Marya's
art and Sandy's . . . Well, who survived? Tell me that?
Who survived — not on obscure discs between thin blue Soviet card-
board, but in real, voluptuous flesh and *blood*. 'I know I done you
wrong.' \No precious attempt to transcend the suffering. No artistic
arrogance. That's it, honey, sing it. Mea culpa. Tell me who's laughing now. And what's the difference between laughing and crying?
Maybe ni kulturni, baby, but who survived?
Who has guys coming all the way up from San Jose to see her? She
could have made it big, but she had a humility. The guys would tell
you about how she had a spot on Ed Sullivan and a contract with
Columbia. She turned it all over to come back to the Dennyman. And
now if her sets weren't what they used to be — Marya Terazinya forgive
her — neither were the guys. And who noticed after five vodkas? What
a treat! Admirers after all these years. So tell me, who's the survivor?)

Carol couldn't concentrate. The red light said the records she had not
heard were over. She knew it was ridiculous to romanticise the isolated
artist and the gregarious hack, even more ridiculous to believe she had to
become one or the other. Delusions of despair and grandeur, which was
which? Of one thing she *was* certain — she was a coward compared to
Sandy Samone. She would have *swallowed* the peroxide.
The unshrouded rock flaunted its incompleteness like a SPUC embryo.
Stark. Demanding. She could find no distance from it. She felt like she
was tottering from adolescence to menopause, in a coma of glandular
fever. But there were supposed to be stages of relative sanity in between.
In between. Two many curves. Too many corners. It was the straight
edges. The bottom, the beginning. The very base.

('Tell our listeners, Ms Thompson, to˙ what do you attribute your
drive? How did you survive female socialisation?'
'Survive, did you ask?'
'Yes, how did you survive the stereotyped conditioning? Many of the
women in our audience, of the same age as you, are undoubtedly
wondering how. . . . '
'Georges Sand decided at 27 that she was either going to be sane or
crazy.'
'Perhaps we could go to a more specific question.'
'Don't you see, it's all a choice. To be mediocre or_____. You either
_____ or you don't.'
'Yes, umm, well, if we could go back to your work. How did you
rationalise your political and aesthetic priorities?'

'You don't get it. It's all a choice. Not to separate thought and feeling and action. That's what aesthetic . . . that's what survival is. You don't get it, do you?'

'Carol, you really do need a rest. Get away for a while. Don't worry. It was only a taped show. Only a few women in the audience.')

'Damn telephone,' she put down the hammer and walked over to answer it. 'Damn telephone at 4 o'clock in the bloody morning. You're never completely free.'

'Carol Thompson? Yes, this is Carol Thompson. Rape Crisis? Yes. Yes. Put her through now.'

'WHEN did it happen and ARE YOU OK?'

'How do you feel now?'

'No, it's NOT your fault. Get that idea out of your head right away.'

'So you're going to believe someone who assaulted you in the street? He DOES have an interest in telling you it's your own fault.'

'That's it, cry if you want.'

'And get angry if you want.'

'Of course I want to come to the police station with you.'

'Not the end, yes, that's right.'

'Can't undo it, no but you don't have to *continue* being the victim.'

'Sure, sure, cry if you want.'

'Yes?'

'Don't apologise. We've all got to stop apologising.'

'Yes, of course you should report it — for your own peace — and for other women. You don't want him to do it again. A lot of us . . .'

'To more of us than you imagine.'

'Look, why don't I just come over and we can have some coffee?'

'No, no love, I can't make you go. I don't want to make you.'

'Why don't you just give me your number and I'll ring later to see how you're feeling.'

She didn't sleep herself that night. Six feet of cold stone slept under a different sheet. No, sculpting is *not* like giving birth. The work was not enough, alone. But it was the largest part of her whole. It sustained her like nothing else. And accepting that, there were no more decisions.

'Telephone. Finally.' The low pitched ring continued as she lifted the receiver. She reached over and flicked off her travel alarm clock. 7 am. Drawing the curtains, she was disappointed that the city was fogged in even more than the night before. There was usually some break at sunrise. The temperature must have dropped ten degrees. The frost edged the panes slightly thicker than yesterday. Carol switched on the kettle and turned back to work.

Radio Times
Michelene Wandor

The radio is on a lot. Parsley. Sage, rosemary and thyme are musical in the kitchen. My favourite song three years ago, favourite harmonies. You get hooked into their dream world unless you make a world of your own. And that's hard when there's so much tugging at you — other harmonies, books to be read, big colour epics, fill the screen, your eyes and ears, raisins and peanuts in the aisle, all alone, all secure, not a decision in the world to be made.

●4.20   Tony back from school first, running to beat his younger brother, door kicked open. Spurs bag dumped in the hall pushing the rug askew, race into the kitchen, pink face, hair pushed back by the running wind, he gulps down orange juice. 'Can I have a chocolate milk shake as well?' He sits at the kitchen table to read the sports page in the *Evening Standard*. Already at ten he turns straight to the sports page. 'Mind my work,' I say.

Jimmy, Bert's friend, trots in, straight to the phone to ring his Mum and tell her where he is. Then he comes into the kitchen, takes an apple and says can I drive him home later. No, I lie, the car's broken. Spoilt brat, he only lives up the hill. Jimmy races off to go and play football with Bert who's gone straight to the adventure playground from school. Tony, in a haze of territorial superiority, prepares to enjoy being the only child in the house and switches on the TV for *Jackanory*. From the *Evening Standard* sports page to pre-school tele programmes in ten minutes flat.

Look at Simon and Garfunkel. The hits just flowed, says the invisible man in my small leather and chrome box. When they made their records, did they decide they would be hits? While they cried all the way to the bank, I proof-read other people's books. Two hundred and forty-eight in the last three years. With the radio on. The radio's free. No-one pays me to listen.

•6.00   Bert bursts in, rosy, loud, vest and trousers, shirt tied round his middle, leaves the doors wide open. Streaks of mud up his arms, he clutches a wadge of mixed squashed wild flowers. Following more slowly comes Jimmy. The two of them rip up yesterday's paper, wrap the flowers in cornets and go out to sit on the front wall and hawk them to passers-by. Two gullible long-haired girls stop and hand over their 5p. A man ostentatiously crosses the road to avoid confrontation. 'Bollocks,' Bert vibrates down the street. 'Ssh,' I say lamely, 'not so loud,' through the kitchen window. I have scrubbed the potatoes and answered the phone twice.

•6.15   Graham comes in with his bike, wanting a pump to blow up a low tyre. Also can he ring his Mum; when he got home the door was open but his Mum wasn't there and when he went out he shut the door by mistake. Yes, he usually has a key but he left it on the kitchen table when he went in. He rings. It's engaged, he says, he's going up the road to see if she's in the laundrette or something. Tony gets the pump from his bike and pumps up Graham's tyre because he knows how to work the pump best.

•6.30   I put the potatoes in the oven to bake and start mixing the cottage cheese salad. My fourth cup of coffee since they got home. Tony is hovering, trying to get me to play football with him. He gives up when the younger boys promise they'll let him be in goal.

What about all the other listeners? How do they make their decisions? 'Scarborough Fair.' That was the name. I always think of it as 'Parsley, sage, rosemary and thyme.' Lyrics matter a great deal to Paul Simon and Bob Dylan. Jesus. Bookends. Fabulous LP. Remember listening to it on Radio Luxembourg, Christmas 1972. Silent evening, kids in bed, before silent night. Sometimes footballs, fights, screams, everything at once. Cool silence now; interruptions can be like scalding water poured in your ears. Someone else decides which record to put on.

•6.45   Graham is back. No Mum in the laundrette. He rings again; still engaged. I suggest walking round there with him and say cheerfully that if she's not back we'll leave her a note with my address and phone number so she knows where he is.

We start walking. Graham wheeling his bike ('just in case'). He must be the same age as Bert and Jimmy. Bert brought him triumphantly home one day shouting, 'Guess what! Gra only lives round the corner and I haven't seen him since nursery school.' Graham is small for eight, pale face, green eyes, heavy hanging dark hair. Quiet and self-contained.

I try and probe as we walk. Has he got any brothers and sisters? No. Does he always take his key to school? Oh yes, but sometimes I forget it. Does his Mum work at home, like me? No, she gets work in all different places. Offices and places like that. She's starting a new job tomorrow and she's going to take me to see a computer.

•6.50   As we turn the corner into the square where Graham lives, we almost bump into a woman coming the other way. She stops and greets Graham. For a second I feel relief to find his mother worried and looking for him.

She's a friend of his Mum's down from Harlow for the day, she comes to London now and again and usually looks Betty up when she's got time. She's carrying a large chocolate Easter bunny wrapped in thick yellow and brown art-nouveau paper. I explain lightly that Graham is with me, and we were just coming to see if Betty was back. 'No, she isn't. I've just tried.' 'Her phone's been engaged for ages,' I say. 'Yes, it's out of order, I had it checked.'

I invite her to come back and wait with us but she looks at her watch and says she'll go back to Betty's house and wait, she's got to catch the 8.00 train back anyway. I write my name and address on a piece of paper and give it to her to leave through Betty's letter box, and Graham and I turn back, me carrying the chocolate bunny. His hands are full of bike.

'Never mind,' I chirp, 'she'll know where you are when she gets back.'

How can you be sure that you have all the evidence, that your decision won't be premature. Every day thousands of tiny decisions get made. And every so often one in the chain heralds the big decision, the important one. A friend of mine is going to China where they don't have Simon and Garfunkel. Maybe she'll pick up a hint or two. Maybe one day we'll all be fitted up with little wires so that every time a really important decision comes up, really important for you and other people, you get a little thrill. Meanwhile, turn the magic knob, Mrs Robinson. Wait for the lies. The lines. Jesus loves you more than you will know, Heaven holds a place for those who pray. Killing me softly with his song. Rhyme. Guitars? argue with the words. Chorus. Put it in the pantry with the cupcakes. She didn't know either. Had to hide it from the kids. Can't let them find you in bed with a strange man. Repent. Secrecy. Lying on the sofa on a Sunday afternoon. Any way you look at it you lose. Christ. America writes the songs, America calls the tune. Sharpen your wits, get in there and fight. Never retire. Decide.

•7.15   Supper is ready, the kids have all been watching tele quietly. Jimmy has waved goodbye and run off. Graham's tyre has wheezed flat again so he's put it round the side of the house. His Easter bunny is sitting on the hall shelf, still wrapped. I ask Graham if he's hungry. 'No, not very.'

Just as I've got the potatoes out of the oven and everything ready to dish up, the Harlow lady rings the bell. Just to say she's got to go now and for Graham to tell Betty she dropped in . No, she can't stop for a cup of tea. Nice to meet you.

We all sit watching the *Virginian*, eating potatoes, cheese, salami, salad. And finally tinned peaches and cream. Graham's appetite stands up well. Tony and Bert are scrapping, Tony niggling — gradually hogging more and more of the table space till Bert explodes in rage and pushes him so he falls over. Then there's a screaming free for all, during which Graham simply observes, and then we're into the denouement of the *Virginian*.

Apart from the one outburst, Tony and Bert don't seem to sense anything out of the ordinary in Graham's presence. Graham looks surreptitiously at his watch now and again, but gives no other sign. I don't know whether to worry on his behalf or not. I've never met his mother, only spoken to her once on the phone. I wonder angrily whether she's had an accident. I play 'Snap' with Graham to pass the time till he looks at his watch again.

Film of the year, The Graduate, *drools the invisible man. Terrific film, great success. Long live America. Pack of cigarettes and a highway. Pittsburg. Four days to hitch-hike, look for Amerika. With a K. Easy Rider has the dream. You look for it and it's following you all the time. It's really a camera wrapped in a dirty raincoat. Look at the scenery, read your magazine. Little red spots in the chutney as you spoon it into the dish. Paprika. Cars on the New Jersey Turnpike all come to look for Amerika, on the east and west coasts, a pilgrimage but there it is sitting on the couch next to you on Christmas night 1972, watching an old American movie on TV, selling you your tube ticket to the next Odeon dream, everywhere you look. The title's a title, the decision's a decision and someone else always makes the right ones. Cupcakes, cornflakes, wrapped in salt beef sandwiches, mustard tastes sharp up your left nostril, but the people aren't as friendly as they used to be, locked behind their glass windows, friendly at the flick of a knob, but they never answer your questions. Too many people.*

•8.00   The evening's very clear and light. Some white wine left at the bottom of the bottle in the fridge. I run Bert's bath. Graham comes into the bathroom as Bert undresses. The two boys pee together. Bert looks at Graham with new eyes: 'You Jewish?' 'No.' So much for the evidence.

•8.40 Tony and Bert are both bathed and in pyjamas, wet edges of their hair dampening their jacket collars. Graham is prowling and we set out again, leaving the bike and bunny. When we've started I realise it's gone quite cold. Graham is only wearing a heavy cotton top and is shivering, his hands stuffed in his pockets, his shoulders hunched. We run the last bit.

When we get near the house Graham puts on a spurt for the last few steps. The first-floor window is dark. Graham says 'She's not back.' Never mind, I say, let's go in and see whether the note is still there. Through the wide entrance door into a huge cavernous hall, painted grotty green, two eleven-twelve year olds lounging on the curving staircase, one saying, '. . . if he does it again, I'll smash his teeth in.'

On the first landing is a brown door, a wide aluminium-silver letter box quite new-looking; a triangle of white paper sticks out of one corner. The note with my address on it. I push the note through so that it falls on the floor. Through the letter box the flat is dark. Graham shows no emotion at all.

'Would you like to come back and stay with us tonight?'

'Yes, alright.'

We walk back more slowly.

'Where does Betty go in the evenings?'

'She goes to see her friends sometimes.'

'What do you do when she goes out?'

'Oh, I watch television till it's all finished, then I switch it off and go to bed.'

'Do those boys live in the house?'

'They live upstairs. I don't like them. They ride my bike.'

'How long have you been living here?'

'About two years. Or three. She's usually back about ten unless she's gone to a party or something like that.'

'What about your Dad?'

'He doesn't live with us.' As if I hadn't guessed. 'I don't know where he lives.'

Friend of mine described the Osmonds as walking vaginal deodorants. Libel or commercial? Last ditch stand to find the immaculate virgins in the hope that they'll have a few new decisions up their record sleeves. Bridge over troubled water, chalked up an incredible record of 106 weeks in the charts, the LP, no record collection is complete without. I do mean complete. Well, I'm left in the blue. Tim Hardin leaves you nothing, Simon (or is it Garfunkel?) leaves you a moment in which to decide, Janis Joplin couldn't wait to decide, Aretha Franklin is deciding. And Roberta Flack. Sail on, silver world. See how they shine. Pure silver strings at the end. Hours of aluminium letter boxes. Catch 22 has passed off the page and into the language.

●8.55 We are just back in time to catch the last five minutes of *The Likely Lads*. I try and explain to the boys that I like it because it reminds me of boys I knew in the fifties who later came back from National Service as though to a foreign country, and for whom creeping suburbia, refained suburban accents, razor eyes behind net curtains, were a defeat. And yet there wasn't anything else. Fit in or get out. Tony, Bert and Graham think the tele's more interesting than I am. Fifties? Eighteen-fifties, asks Tony? I tickle him soundly.

●9.15 Tony and Bert in their bunk beds; Graham in a sleeping bag on a foam mattress. I suggested he took his trousers, socks and shirt off. He doesn't want pyjamas, he doesn't want to pee. Tony throws books at Bert. Bert kicks back. I haul Tony off to the bathroom to tell him to stuff it; he's alright, he's not worried about where his Mummy is. Anyway, he's older. Lights off. Bert says, 'You haven't kissed us.' I do and ruffle Graham's hair.

In the middle of a record there's sometimes a moment's panic, suddenly the congruence is wrong, it jars, is it the music, is it a faulty disc? Sit back and wait, someone has made an arrangement and the next bar comes right. No misunderstanding if you work your way through it.

The rest of the evening I sit, within hand's reach of the phone, waiting. The television is on. Worrying about whether to worry, I can't work. The proof galleys lie splayed on the couch next to me, a biro waiting in case I change my mind. I decide to wait an hour before deciding whether to ring the police. As the late news drones brightly on, a faceless Betty speaks to me through the shape of the newsreader: He's perfectly alright on his own. He can get his supper, put himself to bed, he's perfectly alright in the flat on his own. There's plenty of neighbours if there's a fire. Who can afford babysitters? I hate being a temp. I hate those men who think you're easy just because you move around from office to office. They don't know it's because you can't stand to see their flabby faces, all like each other, it's just the change of background you do it for, not the *people*. It pays better, that's why. What I do in the evening's my business. He's healthy and happy, isn't he?

I wait another hour.

●12.30 The tele whines facelessly. No-one has rung. No-one has come. Graham is sleeping restlessly, talking in his sleep, can't make out the words. He gets up to pee but isn't really awake.

•1.00   I go to bed. There is no such thing as a good mother. I leave my door open 'just in case'.

When a record hushes round and round, the needle caught up in the smooth circle in the middle, you remember other music. Springtime three years later things jump unbidden to the top of your mind, the word Christmas is hazy and you can't remember why it stuck. When my children grow off and leave me, I may be like all those other mothers, lines round the eyes and where I used to smile. There will be no-one to need me.

Next morning Tony and Bert go to school, after an argument as to which takes dinner money in silver and which takes it in copper. Silver is favourite, because that way there are fewer coins to lose. Graham's school has half term this week.

•9.00   I suggest that we go round to Graham's house but he says that if she's back she won't like getting up before ten o'clock. What about her new job? Oh, she doesn't start that till Monday.

•10.00   We walk round the corner again. It is sunny. My proofs must be finished and delivered tomorrow. My working day without my own children is not available to be filled with other people's children. We reach the house. 'She's back.' The window is shut, the curtains drawn.
    Graham runs up the stairs and shouts through the letter box: 'It's me, Graham, I forgot my key and — ' The door opens and a bare arm leans out, followed by a head, the same dark hair, green eyes smudged with mascara. The rest is hidden, there is other movement in the background.
    Graham blurts about the friend and the bunny and I explain that I'm a friend's mother and Graham stayed with us because he shut himself out and didn't know where she was. I'm beginning to feel like a social worker. I'm afraid she'll see what I was thinking last night. Graham says can he go back with me to get his bike and bunny and she nods yes and gives me a big smile.

In two years time I may remember 1975 as the year the United Nations told us was International Women's Year, the year Helen Reddy had a hit called 'Angie Baby'. This girl lived shut in her room, in the world of her radio. A boy who tried to make her disappeared into the sound of her radio and was never seen again. One American TV network said Helen Reddy had to either shave her armpits or tape over her nipples before she appeared on tele. She shaved. I wonder what made her decide that way.

Graham skips along, criss-crossing the pavement in front of me. I'm also walking faster. 'I'm glad she's in a good mood, sometimes when she's tired she isn't in a good mood.' 'Yes,' I say, 'I'm like that sometimes when I'm tired, aren't you?' But of course that isn't what he's saying.

•10.20   Back at the house he gets the bike, balances the bunny under his right arm and is off. 'Goodbye,' he says. 'Goodbye,' I say. 'See you.'

Oh, and did I tell you about the time my eldest son broke his finger? Between Christmas and Easter 1974. Well, not exactly broke; more like a crack, a hairline crack in the bone. They heal up in no time, kids do, said the young doctor trying to ignore me and be friendly to the child. Bitch of a sister mistook me for an anxious mother. Sail on, silver world.

•10.30   I stand back for a minute. I must sort out the dirty washing and then get back to picking my way carefully through other people's words. I turn the radio on.

Time, Gentlemen
Michelene Wandor

He had just raised his second pint to his lips when his elbow was sharply jogged. Reflexes jumped and his arm shot out — but not before some beer had spilt on his sleeve, and some more onto the man now perched on the next-door stool. 'Sorry, mate, my fault,' said the man. 'Have the next on me.'

He smiled forgiveness, put the glass down and tried to sponge the beer marks off his shirt cuff. 'Your trousers okay?' he asked the man.

'Oh, nothing, working gear. Seen more beer than soapy water, eh?'

The two men drank their beer in silence. A game of darts was starting on the other side of the public bar, and the man waved periodically to the group of men gathered round watching. One called at him — 'Coming over?' and he gestured back with his full pint to indicate 'Later'.

'You play darts?' the man asked.

'Now and again. I've seen you play — you're in the darts team?'

'That's right, that's right. Regional champions last year. Going to have a fight to keep the cup this year; half the blokes have left.'

'Oh?'

'Yes. Nearly dropped out myself early in the year.'

'Why's that, then?'

'Oh — trouble. You know. Not here — good place, this, landlord here since I can remember. Other trouble. Seen you around now and again.'

'My local now; I was born here, but I haven't lived here for years.'

'I know what you mean. Can't stand being in one place for long, but I always come back here. My missus, she's from the North. Never been able to settle here. Always used to be on at me to move back to her place, but I like having my home here — somewhere to come back to.'

The man finished his drink and in response to another shout, slid from his stool, shouted at the landlord for two more pints 'one for my friend here' and went across for an impromptu darts game.

He sat watching the darts game, early evening enclosing him in a haze of thought. She'd be sorry when she found out about Lorna. Dog-eared it may have been, but his address book still held goodies. Even after two years. Why had she done it? Why just hang up the phone? He tried to retrace the conversation — Lorna had asked him if he would go with her on a pre-publicity tour for the book. It wasn't a big thing, just a couple of weeks round the country, recalling the student days when the student movement circus had travelled the universities of the country, speeches and meetings during the day, parties and different women every evening. All laid on. Not that things were the same any more, but Lorna had kept in touch over the years, to gossip about her love life, to ask solicitous questions about the book now she was working as a publisher's editor. Keeping her oar in. They had never gone to bed together, but he hugged the memory of a party some years before when rosy with drink she had kept falling against him, her breasts cushioning the fall for both of them. Promises, Penny called Lorna's falling about. He had told Penny with a kind of subdued excitement that Lorna had asked him to go on the tour. And she'd hung up, just like that. He'd phoned back immediately; no reply. He tried twice more that evening. No reply.

The man came back to take a long swallow from his pint. 'Nearly back to me old form. Good game. Your shirt alright?'

'Fine. Bit damp.' He hitched his jacket sleeve up to show a damp cuff. He caught sight of his watch. Still only seven o'clock. The pub was losing its opening spruceness, faded red plush against oak panels, twin wall lamps with fringed shades planted round the walls, soft lighting reflected on the engraved glass panels in the windows. The bar was beginning to be punctuated by small groups of figures, mainly men, some women seated round the wall tables, a haze of bluey-grey smoke clouding the air, bursts of conversation drifting. He thought he had arranged to get to Lorna's at eight-thirty. Come over and discuss the book, she'd invited. Dinner? It had taken him half an hour to decide what to wear. If it wasn't for bloody Penny he'd be sitting watching the early evening movie on tele with Nicky. Bitch. She could get in touch when she was bloody ready. She should know his phone number by now.

'Fancy a game?' the man was asking.

'No, no thanks, maybe some other evening.'

'I'm not in your way?'

'No, no, of course not. Like another?'

'Decent of you. You look like I've been feeling — don't mind my saying so. Have I had trouble.'

'Oh?'

'Yes. 'Course, I've made up my mind now, so I feel better in myself. Woman trouble. You know.'

He nodded. The chord of recognition struck, he smiled in sympathy at his own problem.

'Some would say I was well rid of her. But nineteen years, kids nearly grown up, it's not easy.'

'How long have you been on your own?'

'Well, she went about three weeks ago. But I've made up my mind now. What's your line of work?'

'Bit of everything — some teaching, journalism — I'm writing a book at the moment, about pop groups and touring, that sort of thing.'

'My missus was always the one for books. I've put my armchair in front of the bookcase; can't stand the sight of them now. Is it right what they say about these pop groups, women, drugs and that?'

'A lot of it, yes.'

'I said in the end she should go. Packed a case and went down to her brother's for a bit, get a bit of air between us. Daughters both at college now.'

'Yes, you need space.'

'I suppose you must travel round quite a lot, eh? My work's taken me all over the place. Away for months sometimes. She moaned every bloody time. Perhaps I should have taken a bit more notice. Don't suppose you've got much worry in that direction.'

'No-one's immune to that sort of trouble.'

'That why you're looking so, well . . . '

'Yes, yes, I suppose it is.'

'You married?'

'No.'

'Girl-friend left you?'

'Well, not exactly.'

'Don't mind my asking, do you?'

'No, it's a bit hard, though.'

'I know what you mean. My friends all sort of knew, but I never talked about it to no-one. It's different now I've made up my mind. I'm seeing her Sunday, I shall tell her then, she's got to make up her mind, it's him or me.'

'She's got a kid.'

'Divorced, is she?'

'Not exactly.'

'You don't want to mess with married women. Trouble all round, that.'

'No, she's never been married. She's got a kid, eight, he is. Works and supports the two of them.'

'Independent, eh? You know, I thought at first maybe the old woman was on a bit of this independence lark, women's lib and that, getting a bit of her own back. She met this chap at bingo — I ask you, what sort of a man is it goes to bingo?'

He ordered another two pints to a nod of agreement from the man. What hurt most was not seeing Nicky. He didn't know if he was hurt or angered by Penny, or both. He'd once told her that he'd learned more about himself through their relationship than in the whole of the last ten years.

She had roared with laughter, much as she did in the early months of their relationship whenever he tried to tell her that he thought he loved her. She didn't use words like that any more, she said, she didn't believe in it. Okay, he said, what about Nicky? Oh, I love Nicky, she'd said, he's my son, I love him. He's the only person I love. Mad beautiful woman, he'd said, and they'd tumbled back into bed. Two years. His life had changed. He had never been so involved with a child before — personally, that is. Teaching in school was different. Oh, he'd fucked women with children, he prided himself that whatever else, he wasn't prejudiced — all sorts, pretty, plain, blonde, brunette, married, single, even one or two he suspected were also gay. He just liked sex. What was wrong with that.

Penny guffawed at that too. Who didn't, she said? And if he was that cool about it, she said, why did he go to such lengths to flatter women, emanate unspoken promises, hang on their every word when he spoke to them, allow them to flatter him in both the old-fashioned fluttering ways and the new tough sexual equality way. He couldn't help it if he was taller than most women, he said, he couldn't help leaning over women when he spoke to them. He liked women's smells, their bodies, the excitement of different shapes, different bedrooms on cold spring mornings. Chance would be a fine bloody thing, scoffed Penny, equal opportunity would be a fine thing, sex is one thing for single people, a whole other thing if you have kids.

The beer had almost disappeared in the silence. 'I get to hate closing time. I reckon the budgie's lonely, even. I won't wait forever. Have to look round for another woman if she don't decide quick.'

'Well . . . '

'I've given her every chance, mind. I got wild when I found out she was seeing him. I'd been away, on a building job, I couldn't stand being cooped up in a factory job, and there he was. I come back unexpected, I went for him. Knocked him down, no worse but she got mad. Then she got quiet. I'm a strong man really, but this has just about broke me wide open. They're all the same, bloody women.'

'They're not, though.'

'Well, your own woman is different. Another?'

Two more pints ordered. The man drank, then, distracted by a burst of raucous laughter from the dartboard, gave him a pat on the back, asked him to keep an eye on his beer and wandered towards the gents, stopping along the way to greet other regulars. He looked at his watch. Eight o'clock. Still time.

He had soon seen something of what Penny meant. Chubby Nicky, away at the seaside with his grandparents when he and Penny first met. They had spent an Easter fortnight of school holidays in bed, his flat, her flat, eating, reading, seeing films, making love (silly phrase, Penny had said). Occasionally they would watch with defiant self-indulgence as other workers trudged morning and evening into the maw of the underground opposite Penny's flat. He liked teaching because of the long holidays, she taught because it was the only job that would roughly fit in with Nicky's school day.

After a fortnight Nicky had come back. Six years old, a battered suitcase and a huge Teddy called Beddy. As the child burst in, he had tried to flatten himself against the wall. The child had looked him over and then ignored him for the rest of the day, talking only to Penny, demanding the whole of her attention. He felt like a Peeping Tom. He had not touched Penny all day, feeling that Nicky would mind. That evening after Nicky had gone to sleep he had suggested going out for a drink, suddenly wanting to throw off the domestic claustrophobia. Penny gestured towards Nicky's half-open door. 'I can't, I can't leave Nicky. You go if you want to.' 'No, no, I'll bring some beer back', and even the short walk up to the pub and back had lightened the weight for a moment.

The next few weeks were whirling, unsettling, all-absorbing. Penny survived, just, on what she earned. She could not afford babysitters, she would not leave Nicky alone. Nicky constantly interrupted the fierceness of their sexual-overtoned political and intellectual arguments, clutching himself onto Penny's lap, talking shrilly into her face, forcing her to make choices as the two males competed for her attention. He watched, trying to understand how Penny could be these two people, a fierce and loving mother, and a spiky vibrant woman. Memories of moments of her body would dart uninvited into his head at utterly irrelevant times — buying a ticket on the tube, children in the playground playing 'catch'.

From Nicky's first night back, at first every night without fail, a small figure in pyjamas clutching Beddy would blunder into the room and climb into bed with them. It either flopped on top of the blankets, or forced its way in between the two of them. It slept with luxurious abandon, thrusting its limbs everywhere, wriggling and never letting go of Beddy who took up almost as much room on the pillow. Penny somehow managed to sleep through it all, but he, woken up from the moment the child appeared, retreated to the edge of the bed, to the wall, protecting his balls from the child's legs. One night, poised for what seemed hours over the gap between the bed and the wall he had thought 'fuck this' and sat up, a naked shivering figure at the end of the bed. Penny had woken and burst out laughing to see him, and then Nicky had woken up and said in surprise, 'Can you sleep sitting up?' They all giggled, then they all had tea and toast, and he took Nicky back to bed, telling him a story. From then on Nicky came in more rarely, and when he did, left Beddy behind him. Penny got a funny sort of pleasure out of his discomfort. She said he sailed through life being good at everything he touched. It was good for him to see how the other half lived.

The man came back, letting out an involuntary belch. 'Oh, yes, I'll soon be back on form again. I want to forget it all as soon as possible. It'll be good to have proper meals again.'

'You don't cook?'

'Nah. That's a woman's job, isn't it? I don't know, she's a good girl really. It got me that all the neighbours knew, before me. I mean I've been around a bit, you know what I mean, but it's always been away, it's not as though any of the family or neighbours knew the women. It's quite a different thing.'

'I like cooking.'

'Well, takes all sorts. A pie's enough for me, I can manage on my own.'

Two more pints arrived.

'Women like cooking more than men anyway,' the man said.

'Mine doesn't.'

'More fool her, then, eh? No offence.'

It wasn't as though he hadn't changed; apart from one or two fleeting sidelines in those early months, they were what was known as monogamous. Not on principle; but that's how it worked out. Penny said she had all her energy cut out keeping going, managing Nicky's demands and her relationship with him, she had no time for playing sexual games with anyone, male or female. That was the privilege of childless people. They had choices. She didn't. That was when he called her a puritan, said socialism didn't mean people having tabs on people; no, she said, that's right, she said, but I am not a person, I am a walking relationship, I am a mother, love me love my Beddy. Why should I lend support to other people's sexual freedom while I'm busy bringing up the next generation of good non-sexist socialist? Kill-joy, sour grapes, he taunted. Bloody right, she said. Where's my support? Out of sight, out of mind. We'd never have met if Nicky hadn't gone off with his Gran. Good old nuclear family. When did any of my feminist or socialist friends last offer to take Nicky out in the holidays? Or babysit? No wonder bloody women are backward and politically inexperienced. We can't get near where it's happening. You're a bitter cactus, he said, you don't let anyone near you. Bloody right, she said, you defend yourself your way and I'll defend myself mine.

'I'll give her two weeks,' said the man. 'I've got to think of myself, haven't I? I think I'll put the books in the girls' room so's they won't remind me of her.'

The darts board was taken over, the regular players over in the opposite corner of the bar.

'It's not easy, these days.'

'Well, I'll tell you, what women need today is some good old-fashioned horse sense; know who's boss. If she comes back I won't let her out of my sight. I'll tell her Sunday. Two weeks, I'll give her. By golly I miss her. Nineteen years, eh?'

Penny could be very cold, very hard. Sometimes turning her back on him in bed, sometimes shutting him out. Sometimes it was something he'd done or said, though he didn't always know what, sometimes he just didn't know. She would sob silently, dry, wracking sobs, like an abandoned child in a supermarket. He would stroke her back gently, wanting to comfort, frightened to intrude. He could not always tell how much he was to blame, what he could do about it. In the light of morning she would call him male chauvinist for thinking he could solve the world for her, that he could 'make' her happy; and yet she still said it was his fault. He did not always understand.

'You know, sometimes I wish I could have a really good cry, the missus can turn the taps on like a flood, you know, always could. I can't remember the last time I cried.'

'Big boys don't cry.'

The man splurted laughter into his beer. 'That's a good one, I must remember that one. Big boys — ' And he hooted away again.

A bell rang. He looked up. The landlord, sporting a handlebar moustache and balancing some dozen glasses on the fingers of one hand was shouting, 'Time, gents, please, drink up now', as he collected glasses. He looked at his watch. Eight o'clock. He looked up at the clock. Eleven o'clock.

'This is the first evening I haven't sat here watching the hands creep round to eleven. I hope you don't —'

'No, no, it does you good to talk now and again.'

Making promises, Penny would have called Lorna's voice on the phone. Warm, inviting, dinner, he hadn't turned up. His first date for two years — the movement around the bar lifted his attention away from his timetable. The lights were being switched off. The man slipped off the stool. 'See you again, eh, have a game of darts next time?'

'Yes, sure.'

He got up as well, leaning on the stool. He must have been sitting down for nearly four hours. Always could hold his beer.

Outside the two men stood staring at each other, swaying slightly, both with small smiles of confidence on their faces. The man came close to him and took his hand.

'Good luck, mate, I hope it sorts itself out, whatever it is.'

'And you.'

The man carefully turned round and made off down the road, and he turned the other way, following a trickle of late leavers. A shout stopped him: 'What's your name, mate?' He turned, but couldn't see the man. Perhaps it wasn't aimed at him. He turned back, and carried on home. Equals, Penny had said. People had to conduct their sexual relationships on the basis of equality. But on whose terms, he asked the Belisha beacon on the corner of his road.

You Only Have to Say
Zöe Fairbairns

She couldn't tell him about the fantasy, because then it wouldn't work. She couldn't ask him to rape her, because then it wouldn't be rape.

Besides, she knew exactly what the reaction would be. He would cease to be her friendly husband and become instead her father-confessor and her judge. 'And how often do you find yourself wishing for such an extraordinary thing?'

'Oh, not often, Alec. About three times a year, if that. Usually half way between my periods, I don't know if that's got anything to do with it. Sometimes my months are quite smooth, there's hardly what you'd call a cycle at all. But some months, I feel a sort of inner simmering, it starts maybe only a day or so after the last blood of the last period, and it builds up in the days that follow, till round about mid-cycle my whole body is choked and congested with sex; and it's not a nice loving feeling, either, Alec, not what I really feel for you; it's savage and tearful and shot through with an anger to hurt and be hurt.'

'Yes,' he'd say. 'Go on.'

'I look at men I've known for years as friends, and wonder if I could get them to seduce me. Or I think of men who've been horrible to me in the past, and I want to get in touch with them.'

Even if she said all this to him, it would never occur to him to feel threatened by it. His attitude to hypothetical infidelity was quite simple; he didn't know how he'd react; he'd deal with the problem if and when it arose; but was it worth the risk?

And most of the time she knew it wasn't. They'd been together five years, and she was still incredulous that she could be so content with one person. She'd assumed that once the novelty wore off she would stop being excited by his most casual of touches, that they wouldn't bother to meet each other for lunch when they were both in town, that a dignified and equal friendship would replace the giggling delight of early discovering what it was like to live together. She'd been wrong. Everything got better and nothing became routine. They were ideally suited; everyone said so, and, the important part, they knew so.

'And these fantasies, these rape fantasies . . . ' he'd say.

And she'd tell him (if the conversation ever got this far, which it wouldn't simply because she knew what he would say), she'd tell him all about the faceless rapist with the body like his, who flings her on the bed (it's always the bed; don't want a cracked vertebra on top of everything else) and pulls off her blouse — ripping it — and gives a sort of gasp at the beauty of her bust, and then pulls off his pants, and hers, ignoring her protests, and all the time there's this fierceness born of uncontrolled desire for her beauteous body, and the gentleness that makes her know she need only pretend to be afraid, for he won't hurt her, not really . . .

'It's quite natural,' he'd say, 'in this society.'

Alec taught sociology at the university, and had to read a lot of books about feminism. Also, a lot of his friends and colleagues were in women's lib, so she was in the funny position of having a husband who was a women's libber when she wasn't. She agreed with equal pay and abortion and everything; she just didn't really want to join women's lib, because the books and magazines Alec brought home gave her the impression that she would then have to call all other women Sister and talk in ridiculous detail about orgasms and make love in particular ways and go along with them in the way they thought up involved, political explanations and alibis for things whose explanations were already obvious, or which required none. It was all too humourless and hard-working as far as she was concerned.

Alec would say: 'It's quite natural in this society for women to fantasise about being raped. Women in this society are brought up to feel guilty about screwing, but if you're being raped, you're not responsible, so you don't have to feel any guilt.'

'But I don't feel guilty about screwing!' She'd cry. 'I never have!'

'Not consciously, maybe,' he'd say, meaningfully, falling back on the traditional cop-out of people who make a science and therefore a living out of explaining other people's behaviour. 'Anyway,' he'd add, 'don't feel guilty about the fantasies.'

Sometimes she thought she had found an explanation that did make sense. Part of her wanted a child. The rest of her knew that it wasn't on, because neither she nor Alec wanted the commitments and restrictions it would involve. They reviewed the decision quite often, and always confirmed it, and she knew that it was the right one; yet still she sometimes wanted to be pregnant. It was out of the question, though. An accident was impossible, and she'd never dare cold-bloodedly commit herself to conceiving (with or without Alec's agreement). So . . . just as you wish someone would push you into the swimming pool when it looks

too cold for you to dare, just as you long for someone to hold you down
and yank off the plaster that you are slowly agonisingly pulling away from
the wound, so maybe you dream of rape, to enable you to have a baby
without the burden of deciding to do so . . . well, it was a theory, anyway.

But it didn't explain everything. The rape dream was only part of it.
Sometimes she thought herself into other roles: like being a prostitute,
and having the whole act mean nothing; or being a virgin again, with her
masterful first lover; or even being a man; or being the queen, or a
friend, or someone a different shape or different colour or age, just to see
how it felt . . . she read *Forum* once, and her mind reeled. Did people
really do things like tying each other up, and beating each other and
putting ice cubes up their bottoms and sitting on washing machines? Did
they actually tell each other their guilty dreams, and act them out
together? Get dressed up and play at rapists and schoolteachers and
animals and butlers and slaves . . . all pretty daft, she supposed, but then
so is sex.

'Tell me about when you lost your virginity,' she says.

'I have. Lots of times.'

'I know, tell me again. Were you frightened?'

'No, should I have been?'

'Women often are. Was she?'

'Not that I noticed.'

*Why don't you ask me about when I lost mine? Why don't you ask
me, ever, the deep peculiar questions to which my fantasies are the
answer? And then, when I stumble over the words of telling you,
embarrassed or not understanding myself, why don't you cajole me, bully
me, persuade me to strive to tell you —*

He starts to cuddle her. She feels her insides go all warm. She pretends
not to respond.

'Are you tired, love?' he says.

'No, I'm just not in the mood.'

'Oh. OK, then.' He would respect that, of course. And he settles his
arms round her, to cradle her to sleep.

She grits her teeth. 'Of course, I am open to persuasion . . .' she
mutters, carefully self-mocking.

'Oh,' he says, brightening, 'are you . . .'

'Or even compulsion . . .' she whispers.

'What?' He is shocked by what he thinks he heard her say.

'Oh, nothing.' She kicks his shin.

'What was that for?'

'Nothing, I felt like it, have another one.'

'Look, lay off, that hurts.'

'I'm sorry.' She really is. 'I'm sorry. I was only playing, I didn't mean to hurt you. I didn't, did I? I am sorry.'

'It's OK, you lunatic,' he says, and cuddles close to her, holding her tighter and closer until there is nowhere for his cock to go except into her. *Too soon* she screams silently, *too soon*, then smiles wryly in the dark at the idea of telling a rapist he has come into her too soon . . . 'That's so nice,' she says, and it is; 'Oh yes,' he says, shifting as if to explore every last corner of her insides; he grows tired, they change positions; they have their pleasures, they share them; they lie down to sleep, damp and floppy.

She says, 'D'you think you'd fancy me if I wore a scarlet satin nightie with windows in it for my bum and tits, covered in black lace?'

'I *fancy* you already, if you insist on the term.'

'Yes, but you know.'

'You're not an object to be gift-wrapped, love.'

'Or if I put on my old school uniform.'

'What do you think I am?'

He drifts off to sleep. She lies wide-eyed and embarrassed; her blood beginning its simmering.

She woke next morning with the dull pain of her lust grinding in her gut. She went to work and was light-headed and flippant with the male workers. She even thought she might be smelling of her desire. She began to realise she had to do something about it, kill it or cure it. She thought of Sean who had lured her at sixteen, with promises of love, money and carnal delight, to submit to his thoughtless and masterful embraces, and whom she had seen perhaps a dozen times in the intervening ten years, usually by chance; who always made it clear he'd be glad to have her again, given the option, but wasn't too bothered, one way or the other; and whom she had never quite managed to tell to get out of her life, despite not liking him much, because of the constant feeling that she might one day want him again, if only to lay (so to speak) his own ghost.

She phoned and arranged to see him. She said she'd go to his place. It was as if he'd been expecting her call and wanted there to be no misunderstanding as to his reasons for giving her his time. She wondered all afternoon what the hell she thought she was doing. At the very least, he would screw her and turn her out. At worst . . . still, she would deserve whatever happened. She thought a little desperately about Alec. But he need never know, so it wouldn't hurt him. This had nothing to do with him and her. She had this need, and he couldn't satisfy it, almost by definition. She had to go. She had to sort things out. The decision didn't make her feel any better. All afternoon, she could hardly sit still.

Sean was still tall, dark, and, in a cliched sort of way, handsome. He smiled perfunctorily as he let her into his flat. 'How are you?' he wanted to know. OK, she said, I just wanted to see you, I don't know why. He seemed pleased, curiously enough. He wanted to know about her work, was she enjoying it? And how was Alec? Oh, he was fine, she said, everything was fine, and there was silence. He offered her a drink and then food. She wanted to know if he had a girlfriend, but couldn't ask. He played records they used to know together, and she relaxed in his deep chair, and he sat opposite and watched her with his slightly hooded eyes. She knew that hooded-eye look, in a minute he would pounce; she tensed for him; he said, it was nice of you to come and see me. I wanted to, she said, it wasn't a question of being nice, I think of you a lot. Does Alec know, he said? No, she said. Would he know if we, you know, saw each other often? I suppose it would depend how often, she said, once or twice more he wouldn't know. It would be nice, wouldn't it, he said, and moved to the floor by her chair, and knelt up to kiss her cheek. I'm really rather a nicer person than I once was, he says; at least I'm working on it. Well, she says, good, I'm sure you are; I must go and get my bus. Must you? he says; and then, while she looks closely at him, considering whether she possibly can, whether it could possibly be all right, he settles it: '*Please,*' he says, and she hastens away.

Keeping her mind blank, she scurried to the bus, hauling her suddenly weary self up the stairs to smoke. She felt frightened. She kept her eyes off the dark world outside the bus, where every shadow hid a flasher.

A man came up behind her silently in the near-empty top-deck, and sat beside her.

She froze. He didn't need to sit there. He was up to something, and she didn't want to meet his eye. From the corner of hers she knew he was a small slimy little person in his late thirties, tatty and sallow-faced, smelling faintly of curry. He needed a shave. And he was pressing his leg against hers.

No, he wasn't, of course he wasn't, it was her imagination. She shifted about till a few inches separated her leg from his, and got some peace. But why couldn't he sit somewhere else? Well, why didn't *she* sit somewhere else? Because if she said 'excuse me' he would know that she knew that he was touching her up, and the only defence in these situations is to ignore it. What if he didn't move, would the people in the front of the bus help if she screamed, or would they assume she was imagining it, or wishing for it (maybe she was). His leg met hers again. She forced herself to give him a calm, intimidating stare. His eyes met hers, full of innocence as he moved his leg away. She must have been imagining it.

Now he scrabbled in his pocket, fumbling her thigh at the same time. She stared again; his hand went back to his lap, holding a pen.

He started to write something on a bit of paper.

Once when she was a schoolgirl, a man in a public library drew a huge penis and pair of balls on a note pad, caught her eye and showed them to her. She didn't even know what they were, but it scared her. Now she felt the same fear, creeping like tide up her spine, accompanied by hate for the contemptible little man who made her feel so.

Suddenly, he was gone. He raced down the stairs without a word and left the bus. She watched him disappear into the night before she turned to look at the note he had left for her; better not give him the satisfaction of knowing she'd read it.

He had scrawled on the back of the bus-ticket, 'you are Beuatifull Angell'. It was like the writing of a clever six-year-old.

She knew if ever she told Alec, he'd say, male chauvinist pig, harrassing women who have every right to travel on buses alone and late at night if they wish; and it was true of course; but all she could think was, poor little bloke. *you are Beuatifull Angell.* And he doesn't even know I've read it. Back to his greasy bedsit, shared with a dozen other Wimpy waiters, thinking of me, a ship who passed in his night. HMS The Beuatifull Angell. I'm not really, anyway. (Am I?)

She ran home from the bus stop as if a rampaging army was after her. She could see the lights of their home from the bus stop, so she knew Alec would be in, glancing at the clock to check the time when the last bus came, and putting on the kettle.

'Now what is it?' he wanted to know when they were warm in bed and she started to giggle.

'Nothing.'

'Share the joke,' he said, in schoolmasterly tones, and she joined in as he went on: 'Nobody enjoys a good joke more than I.'

'It's nothing.'

He raised himself on his elbow, and looked sternly at her. 'If you don't tell me why you're laughing,' he warned, 'I'll give you something to laugh about.' And, getting no response, he started, slowly, deliberately and purposefully, to tickle her into submission.

'I was . . . I was . . . only wondering,' she gasped, 'how you'd react if I wrote a sexual suggestion on the back of a bus-ticket, and passed it to you.'

'You're insane,' he said affably, and it seemed the end of the subject, but one day soon after he said, 'You are happy with how we make love, aren't you. I mean, if you ever want to do anything different, you know you only have to say, don't you?' and she said, oh yes, she knew she only had to say.

Penelope
Sara Maitland

Once again I can't sleep. I lie gently listening to the sea, the bright blue
Ionian, which turns to the colour of wine in the evening, but by this time
will be becoming greyish green before dawn. Odysseus is sleeping beside
me, his back lifts and falls as smoothly as the sea, a back which says with
every rise and fall, 'I have come home, I have kept faith, I love you,
Penelope.' Of course, like the sea there are storms; sometimes he is
restless, his eyes go roving, but each night his steady breathing confirms
the deepest truth, when every muscle breaths, 'Penelope, Ithaca, my
children, my home.'

I sleep less well than he does; not because I am less contented, but
because I still find it difficult to share my bed. And tonight there is
something more: we had an idiotic minstrel here tonight who sang in
praise of Odysseus. Very seemly, except that instead of singing about the
Trojan war, in which Odysseus played a very creditable role, or about his
diplomatic successes, he chose to sing of how he tricked every attractive
woman in the Mediterranean into bed. The lying and duplicity that he
claimed for Odysseus were somehow to his credit, and far nobler than the
skills he had shown in getting Achilles to fight or planning the Trojan
Horse plot.

We listened in silence to line after dreary line about the physical
charms of assorted women and how Odysseus had got round their
modesty or virtue, and how this was a heroic and thrilling way to spend
ten years. I cannot close my eyes to facts, but that does not mean I like to
hear every detail in public. Odysseus was becoming embarrassed, sheep-
ish which I hate, and he was on the verge of being angry with the singer
which I felt to be unfair and dishonest of him. He, of his own choosing, is
a public figure, his acts are in the public domain. Worse still, the element
in the court that Odysseus calls my 'swains': the young men who grew up
while he was away, grew up with the feeling that he had betrayed them,
and transferred this to a protective passion for me: were beginning to get
restive. As though this were not enough, this insensitive poetaster then

turned his attention, again in Odysseus' honour, to my touching fidelity, my doting endurance. It was unbearable. And my boys began to cheer. There was nothing I could do. I could not leave because of embarrassing Odysseus. It brought us back, once again, to that difficult truth, that I had done better, gone further than he. It is something that we believe we have sorted out for ourselves, but that does not make it free of tension, does not make it easy.

After the infernal meal was over and I, with an appearance of modest virtue, had offered the minstrel his customary wine, Odysseus and I withdrew to our room rather quicker than etiquette allowed.

'I'm sorry,' he said at once.

'I know,' I said; there was nothing else to say.

After we had made love and the tension eased, he asked me,

'Where did this preposterous habit spring from? Do you think anyone could enjoy having their more sordid exploits mauled over in public?'

'Yes,' I said, 'people really do. Look at my family. They'd have loved tonight, both the tension in the hall and the thought of their fame. Helen would love to hear songs about how her adultery dominated the population of Greece.'

'And it was all our fault.' The evening had clearly upset Odysseus badly.

'Nonsense,' I said sharply, although I have never been absolutely sure. The idea brought back the horrible weeks of Odysseus' breakdown before he had sailed for the Trojan war. That is one place I am not yet brave enough to go again.

'It's not nonsense, dearest. We knew what Helen was like and we entangled Greece in her marriage stability, just so we could get married quicker.'

'Just so we could get married at all. Perhaps we didn't have the right to use her like that, and certainly we ought to have guessed she would be bound to indulge some casual, selfish whim, but we did our best to resolve an impossible situation. The really sad thing is that she never even loved Paris. Involving every kingdom in Greece, more good men than one cares to think of, dead; and all for a few moments of self-indulgent gratification, because she was bored.'

'From all accounts she was colossally bored in Troy.' I could feel Odysseus' amusement beside me, unlike most men he genuinely dislikes Helen. 'She gets bored at home with her husband and baby — his fault too, of course — and runs off with a smooth talking charmer; she's the centre of attention in two whole countries, everyone ready to die for her, utterly thrilling. But the war discounted her, she became a political pawn in an international power struggle. No one in Troy had much time for her. By the end no one even thought she was worth it. Pathetic.'

'Poor thing,' I said, and tried for a moment to feel what I knew to be true.

We lay together thinking about Helen for a while and then Odysseus said,

'I thought we might take Ptoliporthe up to the cottage tomorrow to visit her grandfather. We could take a look at the new orchard on the way.'

'I ought to be down in the harbour seeing about sail cloth,' I said, 'but it shouldn't take long. Laertes would love to see her.'

'Is she really as wonderful as we think, or are we biassed?'

'Both,' I said. 'She's the child of our dotage, don't forget.'

Odysseus grinned, kissed me and drifted off to sleep.

I lie awake now and listen to his breathing and to the sea. But in the end I get up and wander round the house. I remember how I found it crude and cramped and am amazed now, because I have come to love it. We have been through a lot together, this house and I. Finally I come to the nursery: Ptoliporthe is asleep, she has kicked her blankets off and is lying on her front with her hands tucked under her and her ridiculous bottom stuck up in the air. Daily I am grateful to her and for her. I can't help wishing I'd had a daughter from the start as things turned out. Where a daughter might have grown up more simply as a friend, I know that too often I tried to make Telemachus more than that, some sorts of substitute for his father. But now for the three of us, Odysseus, Telemachus and I, a daughter is perfect; we none of us really wanted another boy. Sentimentality almost overcomes me when I look at her lying here, her blond hair tufting out in little horns where her sweat has dried. I wish though that her hair was dark: she looks too much like my side of the family; not a fate I'd wish on my worst enemy. No one would wish their own child ugly, but that excessive self-justifying beauty seems to stunt a person's growth. I sound like the prude they accused me of being when we were young, but, sweet gods, history has borne me out.

I sit down beside the cradle and fill in the last few hours of the night thinking about this history, trying to make sense of it, trying to find something to tell my daughter, trying to explain to her uncaring sleep how my apparently placid life is in fact a braver, more adventurous choice than the dramas of my famous cousins. How in the end, not without grief and loss, I made the better choice.

My family is quite different from my husband's. Ithaca is a backwood; Odysseus has made a place for himself in political life, but it is not based on the power or importance of his beautiful, impoverished little island. My husband, though loved and raised as Laertes' son, is by common knowledge a bastard. His mother was pregnant when she married Laertes. But the result was Odysseus, and I expect that Laertes would say it was worth having an unfaithful wife to get such a son. At heart Ithacans, even royal ones, are peasants: bred to real things; the sea the land, the simple rhythms of tides, seasons, matings, death. Not that Odysseus is simple, but in the end he really likes raising sheep and improving his fishing fleet, and he has the courage and self-knowledge to do it and enjoy it.

Sparta on the other hand is the centre of the world, or was when I was young. There is, not surprisingly, a doom on the place now. But when I was a child it was the richest, most luxurious court in Greece, and my family one of the most influential dynasties. Perseus was one of my great-grandfathers, another sailed with the Argonauts. The belief that we were descended from Zeus was certainly one of the factors that led to that casual assumption of importance which has affected everything we have done since. By the time I can remember my uncle, Tyndarus, was king, but, apart from depriving them of all responsibility and self-respect, he treated his brothers well and they all remained at court. He married a beautiful, exaggerated woman called Leda and spent the rest of his life trying not to notice what she got up to. They, or rather Leda, had six children, four of whom were quads — Helen, Clytemnestra, Castor and Pollux — and were exactly my age. My mother died in childbirth and my father did not bother to marry again, so we were all brought up together in a royal nursery, pampered, petted and allowed to do exactly what we chose. Later I realised we did what we wanted only because no one cared; but that does not change the fact that at the time it was fun.

It was only as I got older that I began to recognise the disadvantages. The principle one was that there was nothing to do. Nothing. As princesses we could turn our hands to no useful work. That is how the story of my weaving started: I really love to weave, I only learned when I came here, and when Odysseus went off to Troy I wove a great deal; useful things, sheets, covers, sails, yards and yards of creamy, waxy cloth. I liked the rhythm, I liked being together with the other women, and I liked the sense of being part of a necessary production process. When this gossip arrived in Sparta they were so amazed that they dreamed up a whole ridiculous motivation for someone of the Blood Royal undertaking anything as improbable as weaving. But after my childhood I really enjoyed functional work, weaving and farming and rearing my own children and administering our community, creating something real.

We never did that sort of thing in Sparta. Instead the principal lesson of our youth came when Helen was carried off by Theseus, when we were all about twelve. When Helen was brought back she had an odd knowing look and spoke to men in a new way. Thinking about it now I don't believe she slept with him, I think she learned she could humble him by refusing. Afterwards she was treated with a new respect and admiration;

the King of Athens was quite a prize for a pre-pubescent child. The whole incident was made even more exciting for us, because Castor and Pollux were allowed to accompany the rescue party and they came back with adult perceptions about the world of men to which they patronisingly introduced us. Clytemnestra and I were deeply jealous and planned involved seductions and elopements, in which our nurses encouraged us with giggles and shrewd advice. That is how we were brought up; to indulge every whim so long as it was a useless one; to take what we wanted, regardless of the consequences. The boys' games led them to an adoration of casual violence and ours to realise that admiration was both our due and our weapon. We learned that our value lay in the quality of man we could successfully manipulate. Our adolescent practice with grooms and handsome shepherds was nothing but practice and we were encouraged to know it. Sex was never for fun, but for power.

When we were eighteen we moved out into the world and found out what all the practice and training had been for. We were marriageable, counters to be pushed about the political map of Greece, bargaining coinage, worth so much for family and a few additional points for the right sort of personal characteristics. I remember with disturbing clarity the recognition that Tyndarus had tolerated Leda's infidelities because of the high-value, beautiful end-products. Clytemnestra was lovely enough, but Helen . . . Every single thing that any gossip or songster has ever said about Helen's beauty is true, is probably short of the truth. I have seen a number of very beautiful women, in various styles and, simply, there is no comparison. She was a small woman with fine features, and she had extraordinary, unforgettable colouring; silver-gilt hair and unbelievably pale skin, somehow translucent; where the skin went over her eyes it seemed to glow grape coloured, but for the rest it was pale and in summer went the colour of honey. She used to mix gold dust with her face powder, and if anyone else had done it it would have looked bizarre, for her it was a superfluous perfection. She had these immense, improbably black eyes. Leda had an elaborate fantasy that the four of them were the children of a swan: Helen gave the story an extraordinary plausibility. Almost overnight, when we reached the magic age, the court was seething with suitors: every prince in Greece wanted this trophy, this ultimate accolade, proof of his manhood and his social status. The descendent of Lacedamon, the daughter of the Spartan throne, the child of a swan, the humbler of Theseus, the jewel of Greece.

It swiftly transpired that Tyndarus had overplayed his hand. He had built her up as the only acceptable prize for the perfect prince, and now he had to judge at least twenty-five extremely arrogant and powerful young men as imperfect. In the meantime they all hung around, eating his food, drinking his wine and massacring everything that moved on his hills in their hunts. Helen loved the tensions, the excitement, the being the centre of attention. In honesty I admit that I loved it too, what little that rubbed off on me. But occasionally I would get nervous. I remember one evening clearly, when the three of us were sitting alone discussing the day's events, and I said,

'Helen, don't you wish you could get your hands on some of the presents they're giving Uncle? They don't even talk to you, just strut around trying to impress each other.'

'Nonsense,' said Helen crossly.

'It's not nonsense,' said Clytemnestra, her eyes narrowing. The situation must have been painful for her, I realise now. 'You're just a prize in a contest that no one can back out of now, and there you'll be, married off to some rich arrogant pig who'll try and keep you battened down.'

'He can try,' said Helen, 'look, just marrying me will make my husband premier prince of Greece; he won't dare try. I can keep him where I want him. Look at mother and father; a beautiful woman can get anything she wants, if she's clever.'

'But what do you want?' I persisted. Helen seemed so sure of her answers, and I badly needed some of that assurance.

'Oh, I don't know. I want to be important, adored and everything. And I want to be free to choose what I'll do. I want to be famous and have an exciting life, and, well, be on top of things, in control.'

'Yes,' said Clytemnestra, 'that's why we need husbands; a prince to dote on us and give us status, make people respect what you do, and provide the background.' She giggled, 'I can tell you, Helen, I mean to get a husband out of this too. Who do you think would suit me? I rather fancy Meges, very sexy.'

'Which is he?' I asked.

'O Penelope,' they were exasperated with me. I was getting exasperated with them. They did not seem to recognise their impotence. Whatever they said would make no difference; Tyndarus would choose Helen a husband, when he had worked out the political complications, and that would be that. She would move to a different court and carry on as before. I would stay and wait my turn to be married off. There seemed so little point to it all.

I wonder now if these are the perspectives of today; because I also remember clearly that I adored Helen, idolised her and struggled to be like her and thought it unfair that life had offered her so much, while I would have to make do with a second rate prince, as I had been forced to make do with second rate court lovers.

Then everything changed. There was another hunt. A heavy hot day, although still early in spring. The princes strutted round showing off their dogs and horses. There was a great deal of noise. Helen, looking as pale and cool as ever, stood up in the chariot we were sharing shrieking with delight, excited by the blood and baying hounds. I climbed down after a bit, feeling sweaty and inelegant beside her. I didn't approve of hunting during the breeding season and the growing pile of carcasses was beginning to stink. I wandered off by myself looking for some shade. I felt dreadfully, despairingly bored, although I knew so little about myself that I was hardly able to identify the sensation. I dozed off for a little I think, but was jerked awake by the sudden appearance of a young man, one of the princes, a little dark person.

'Who are you?' I asked, feeling foolish. I ought to have known.

'Odysseus.'

Then I did know; he was the prince of some small island state. We had laughed about him because he was so small, and because he had a growing reputation, not for valour, but for intelligence. Helen particularly felt that Real Men should not hesitate to think.

'Why aren't you hunting?' I asked him.

'In Ithaca, where we don't have this profusion of game, we only kill what we need to eat, and certainly never the ones who are going to provide next year's meals. I'm prudish.'

'So am I,' I said, and he laughed not altogether kindly.

'In exactly what way?' he looked at me oddly and I felt confused.

'I'm not sure. My cousins are always telling me so.'

'Are they? Well I wouldn't let anything they say affect you much.' He said it almost viciously, and I rallied him in what I hoped was Helen's style.

'Is that any way to speak of the woman you are hoping to marry?'

'O, I've given up that scheme.' He sounded so disparaging that I felt shocked. His self-esteem seemed inordinate, his sentiments almost blasphemous, so I said,

'That's lucky for you, because you haven't a hope in Hell.'

There was a long pause, and then I said, 'I'm sorry, I shouldn't have said that.' I'd never been so rude to a man in my life and felt embarrassed.

'It doesn't matter. It's true and it doesn't matter. I've seen through that nasty bit of work, your cousin Helen, anyway.'

'What do you mean?'

'I've no time for self-worship. And in her case it's as good as reification. She doesn't even want to be a human being but a jewellery stand, strung with gold and placed on a little pedestal for life. I've no patience with that, and can't afford the gold anyway. What sort of a queen would she make for Ithaca? What sort of a wife for me?'

'Tell me about Ithaca?' I said, because a different look came over his

face when he said the word. But he jutted his chin and snarled,
'It's a small dirty backwood, dear princess.'
'You don't have to class me with her,' I cried, stung, although until that
moment it had been my deepest desire to be classed with Helen in any way.
'No,' he said, suddenly looking at me, 'I don't.'
And he described Ithaca to me, lovely, rocky, impoverished, backward.
He explained how one had to work twenty-four hours a day, to stay alive.
How he knew the name of every citizen and there were no slaves. How the
court was simple, primitive, the palace just a large house, and the
servants over-familiar and out of control. 'My father, Laertes, is waiting
for me to marry and then he will retire to a cottage on a hill and grow
apple trees. We think that a very proper occupation for a king.' I thought
of my uncle growing apple trees in his old age and had to smile. Odysseus
spoke a lot of his father, and with such love and respect, that I could not
help thinking about how we spoke of our parents. I knew I wanted my
children to think of me as Odysseus did of his father.

Some days later I said, 'If I come to Ithaca, I shall expect to work too, not
be set up on that pedestal.'
He said, smiling, 'Dear Princess, I don't think we have a single
pedestal in the whole of Ithaca.'

Another time he said, 'If you come it will have to be forever. For both
of us. There is no court life, you know; there are no mazes to play in with
pretty grooms, there are no pretty grooms. And we won't have time for
those games. You must choose.'
'Yes,' I said, 'I realise that. But you must never hold the pretty grooms
of my past against me.'
We woke up with a start. I almost cried. 'Uncle is never going to let us
marry before Helen.'
'Damn. No, wait, perhaps he needn't know, we'll ask your father.'
I grinned. 'Odysseus, if we ask my father he'll flop a scented wrist at
you and say, "Dear boy, about marriage you'll have to ask my big
brother, but something else now, let me introduce you to the sweetest
thing, a dancing boy, just this absolute moment arrived from Thrace."
Pronounced Thwace.'
'O dear,' said Odysseus, then after a pause he said, 'Well, put your
mind to work, dearest, we can fix Tyndarus.'
We did. Odysseus told Tyndarus that we had a solution to the princes'
problem and we would tell him if we could get married immediately. My
uncle was delighted and agreed to everything. The scheme we produced
was that Tyndarus should announce that Helen was going to choose for
herself, and that before she did so all the princes had to vow to support

her husband against any future assault on her honour — her what? I asked Odysseus privately. It meant that no prince in Greece could risk assault or seduction. Fear and jealousy would control them. As we suggested, Tyndarus announced that Helen had chosen Menelaus and all seemed well. The only problem arose when Tyndarus, faintly suspicious of Odysseus, insisted that he too had to take the oath.

Then, with everyone excited over Helen's grand nuptials, Odysseus and I quietly got married and sailed at once for Ithaca.

It took nearly eight weeks to sail round the southern peninsular and up the west coast. They were not easy weeks, I was both sea-sick and frightened. I began to recognise the enormity of what I had done, leaving a world which for all its limitations was one I knew and had learned the rules of. I had never been on my own before, without a circle of admirers who would condone my most outrageous behaviour, who liked me to be as simple and superficial as I could manage, who never for five minutes would leave me alone with troubling silence. For the first time in my life someone was taking me seriously, and expecting me to take him equally so. For the first time I took myself seriously, and began the embarrassing business of finding out just who I was: not a beautiful rich princess, but a human being who had used other human beings and who had enjoyed being used in return. And for the first time I began the perilous journey into another person: an endless journey that often since I have wanted to escape from into something easier or more dramatic. I know now there is no escape, no courageous escape, from that commitment not to live in isolation, to live as part of a whole, with difficult rights and equally difficult responsibilities. The two journeys matched; the journeys away from the bright superficial soothing contours of the court into unknown seas, to an unknown land, forever. But we found, Odysseus and I, to our relief and pleasure, that the impulse of our heart and gut had been a sound one, we matched well; filled each other out. He was brave in storms which frightened me, but I was better at the calm periods, more ready to be grateful, unready to sail closer to the wind than necessary.

As the weeks passed I was feeling more and more assured, that I had made at least, a possible choice, that I had committed myself to a viable experiment; but when Odysseus standing beside me pointed out a minute crag sticking out of the sea and said, 'There we are,' I could only reply, 'O my god.'

Ithaca was as bad as I had been warned and worse. It was barbaric, insular, savage. It wasn't glamorous or exotic, often it wasn't even fun. I missed the frivolity, excitements, and more seriously the culture, the education, of Sparta, desperately. Most of the people were coarse and when they got drunk far from weeping sentimental poetry into my ears, they laid into each other with swords. The visitors were not dashing princes to be entertained with tasteful flirtations, they were sea-wrecked sailors who got drunk with relief and told stories that were long, complicated and deadly boring.

Ithaca also became my home, the place where I became Penelope, utterly. The place where Odysseus and I set up house and got to work. There were two things we did and they cannot be separated; we struggled to do something more than free our poor sea-battered people from the bitter drudgery of the fight to feed and clothe themselves, we tried to free them to live a larger more richly cooperative life. And this belief came out of our struggle to live together in mutual respect and equality. It is too easy to divide it into an internal search and an external action; you can't do that. The way we saw men bullying their wives and women humiliating their husbands showed us the ways we had to go together; but equally our discovery of the strength that we could have together informed the sort of cooperative state that we tried to work on. Not many people have three years of genuine growth with as much happiness as we did; but it wasn't easy, learning to give up the privileges and even the oppressions which have made life manageable. For me it was a daily fight against my own pettiness, my own habits of sinking into tears and submission when confronted with the least difficulty. For Odysseus it was more a struggle to admit that he was not always right, that he was not the only person in the entire island who was intelligent and capable. And for both of us it was an effort to learn the otherness of each other, that marriage alone was not enough, was hardly even a beginning. But gradually, slowly, we were able to believe intellectually and not just with faith that our love and happiness spread out, ceased to be a private thing, embraced and in return was embraced by Laertes and the baby; the court, where I grew into having friends; the farming community. Even the crops which fed us, were fed by our love. They still are, it was not a casual thing we built in those three years, it was an enduring muscular love.

And then came the news that Helen had run off to Troy with Paris. Odysseus had a nervous breakdown. It was not that he loved me to madness, any more than I went mad without him: we loved each other to sanity, to calm and order against the chaos. What hurt most was the guilt, the realisation that to marry me he'd trapped the whole of Greece into a silly war over a silly woman. He felt unable to blame Helen, who'd done nothing he hadn't done himself. He felt unable to renounce his oath, because the keeping of oaths was the only frail means of stability in the whole anarchic Greek political system; it was on that presumption that we had based our original plan for Helen. For two horrible months he wept and shook and wandered round the rocky shores; he lost weight, he wouldn't shave, he didn't sleep. I even sent word to the Greek forces saying he was mad and couldn't come. But they sent along a ratty little man called Palamedes to check up on the story. He arrived with the foregone conclusion that Odysseus was faking, out of love for me; preposterous romantic notions were running round Greece in Helen's wake. With me he tried to be ingratiating, saying he could easily understand how any husband would do this for so lovely a queen, and trying subtly to flatter the truth out of me. Life with Odysseus had made me impervious to flattery, I told him the truth: Odysseus was sick. Then he tried Laertes, how surprised he was to see the son of such a hero turned coward. Laertes and I got together, clearly Odysseus could make no decisions for himself: we doped him with poppy seed so he'd be too dazed to weep and shoved him on a boat hoping that the pathetic need that the thoughtless heroes at Aulis would have for his intelligence would help him recover. It worked, that's all I can say. It is the only time I have tried to manipulate my husband, I am still not sure it was the right decision and I still hate myself for it. Nor did it make for a happy parting which was something I was going to need in the years ahead.

The waiting. Why did I choose to wait the way I did? I have dwelt at length on the past because that goes a long way to explain why I chose to wait. When we heard the news about Clytemnestra murdering Agamemnon and throwing the whole State into chaos, just to be with her lover, I had proof of how right I had been. I could perhaps have taken lovers with Odysseus here, to talk it over with and judge the consequences, but not in his absence. But even if I had not heard of the extended and bloody consequences of her decision it would have made no difference. I decided from the beginning that I would concentrate until either he came home or I knew absolutely that he was dead. I cannot close my eyes to the fact that he did not concentrate. The best that I can say for him is that he did in the end come home. I don't say that it is different for a man, I don't say that I understand. I do say that he chose wrongly, but I would also say that I had more things to occupy myself with, real things, cycles of seasons, and births and loved ones, whereas he was alone after he left Troy. But although I love him and forgive him, I do not understand, do not condone, do not make excuses for him. I demand of myself that I am strong enough to accept his decision without trying to sentimentalise the fact that I kept my faith and he did not keep his.

Yes, I was tempted, yes I had long periods of doubt and confusion and desire,\but I could see no final reason to take these more seriously than I took the days of simple clarity when I knew he was alive and would come home. I did have other options: I could have gone home to Sparta where I would have been cossetted and set up on the pedestal of 'perfect wife'. I could have given in to a continuous temptation to take one of my young admirers as a lover — although that would have been unfair to Telemachus and would have driven the others desperate with a jealousy that would quickly have become fashionable and destructive. I could have declared Odysseus dead, set Telemachus up as king and become a power behind the throne, but he seemed very young for such responsibility, and I believed that if I was going to be the power I should be seen to be it so that criticism could flow freely and properly. I could have retired into a darkened room and wept for twenty years and gained a reputation for passionate loyalty. I could even have committed suicide and left Odysseus with a reputation for cruel neglect, and a real sense of guilt. I confess that at one time or another I considered all these possibilities and others, but in the end I just waited. Not with the simple devotion of a simple wife, but as a political and emotional decision. Ithaca, which had begun to flourish in the few years we had been together needed stability and peace. I had promised him in Sparta that it would be for ever and the only way for me to grow towards myself was to keep that promise. I did not wait passively, I waited as we had lived together, actively, busily. I learned the problems of state, of crop rotation and agronomics; I learned to keep the Ithacan youth under control without frustrating them; I learned the backroads of physical desire and I learned I was stronger than that. I learned to concentrate not on his absence, but on my love for him and for Ithaca. I waited, that's all.

And then, suddenly he was home. His old nurse woke me in the middle of the night, excited, twittering. I refused to let myself believe her, but I went downstairs. Telemachus was jumping about like a child, as though he had invented the scene himself. I just stood looking at my husband. It seemed so simple and obvious, he was so very much there, I did not even want a drama. He looked a lot older, I know I did too; I just wanted to take him in in peace for a moment or two, and he felt the same. But Telemachus felt disappointed; I am sure he thought we did not recognise each other. He kept saying, 'Oh Mother, don't be so prudish' until it brought back memories that made us laugh. They ruined the quiet solemnity of the moment, and we were in each other's arms. My hands exploring the back of his neck, his tongue testing my earlobes. I began to cry, to my own annoyance, but dear Gods I was so happy. He said the sweetest things to me, that I shall never forget, he said, 'Dearest, at last I can start travelling again.'

I am forty-two years old and beginning to get fat. I have an ordinary sort of life to all appearances, with a husband and a lot of work to do. I have a name throughout Greece, which is a corruption of my truth, but nonetheless some sort of immortality. I have two children whom I love, rather oddly spaced twenty-three years apart, and I would have liked more, but it is too late now. I have a husband, with whom I can still travel adventurously, a husband whose sleep rocks him gently. I have a father-in-law free to die with the integrity he lived with. My baby is stirring for the morning, my vegetable garden is growing. I am weeping sentimental tears with enough self-knowledge to know they are sentimental and enough self-respect not to be ashamed of them. I will justify my life before the Gods themselves.

Epilogue

I don't believe in happy endings any more. I grew up on a diet of romantic historical novels dealing with the Regency era, fifty or sixty of them written by the same woman and all exploring, or I should say stating, the same theme: every woman loves an upper-class sadist, whose kisses on the final page are indistinguishable from orgasm and therefore remove the need for it, whose velvet-gloved fist has never clutched an iron, and the creases in whose trousers owe something to nurture but even more to nature. Our heroine, hitherto emancipated and chaste (curious how some feminists connect these adjectives similarly), can swoon into his wealthy and eternal embrace because she knows that falling in love is about losing your mind and therefore taking no responsibility for your actions. Madmen must be humoured. When your ribs are being crushed as ferociously as that, perhaps the flow of oxygen to the brain cuts off, anyway. Happy endings of such literally breath-taking simplicity gradually became suspect when I looked at my own life and that of other women, and the contradiction yawned between the words on the page of the dream I was buying and the unspoken words in our heads of the reality we were living and our relation to it. The women's movement jumped into that contradiction and started building a way forwards out of it, and the sadist started making his own bed and lying on it alone.

I don't believe in endings any more. But nor do I agree that only the journey and not the arrival matters. An emphasis on endings suggests a static and not a dynamic view of life; an emphasis on journeys simply exhorts us to try harder. One of our discoveries as feminists and as socialists has been about the nature of change, how the future can only be built from the now, from an acceptance and an exploitation of the two-way connection between ourselves and the world we are part of. Those contradictions we and other women found ourselves living at a particular historical time propelled the women's movement into being. Those of us who were trying to earn part if not all of our living by writing had to start thinking about the connection between our politics and our particular work; between who we were discovering we were as people, and how we were represented in the fiction of a male-dominated culture; between the levels and areas of experience that we considered it politically important to speak about and personally impossible to ignore and the hierarchy of acceptable subjects of writing that began and ended with man pitted against the universe. Yes, we are part of a literary tradition of writing by women, one of whose strands, to pick up on the novels I mentioned above, extends from Mary Shelley's *Frankenstein* through the Brontes and faintly into *Woman's Own* serials. We handle our heritage with affection if with care. Yes, we are historically placed to take that tradition onwards; although bounded by our century and our class, our imaginations speak not only of that which is, but also, moving on from there, of that which we think possible. Not in the romantic sense of fantasy, of science-fiction super-heroines, but in the sense of prediction, using a carefully gained knowledge of the present in order to push forwards into the future. No, we are not unique; we represent only a fraction of the women all over the country who are coming together in groups to leap forward from the isolation and social silence of the diary and the shopping list and the backs of envelopes in order to communicate to others via the alchemy of fiction the concerns of their lives as women and as feminists. All that does not glitter is not necessarily dross. New images please.

I think that our book, besides offering you a good read (for an amplification of the shorthand see the other essays in the book), implicitly does something else. It demonstrates the collective process. In one way obviously; fifteen short stories by five feminists are what you have just waltzed or waded through. But the stories, the print on paper, do not themselves tell you about our relationship to each other and to the project of writing the book.

I feel that we have worked well and successfully as a collective. We knew why we were together; we had a specific project to work on together: producing this book. A solid base from which sprang our commitment to each other as workers and comrades. This commitment to the work and to each other was facilitated, I think, by the small and constant size of the group. We had the time to get to know one another's work over a period of eighteen months and we also recognised that our being one specific group was not exclusive in terms of preventing other women getting together as writers to work in similar or different ways. We came together as equals, defined as such not by some defensive rhetorical statement but by the reality of having all worked previously as writers in some capacity; and I think that this helped too. These factors helped us both to give and to receive criticism as well as affirmation and praise, to argue about the work produced, the ideas informing it, the politics towards which it was directed. Asking each other to rewrite, to reshape, we were continually reminded that manuscripts do not spring unsolicited from the head of a solitary genius in a garret at four in the morning; our domestic lives forbade the experiment anyway, and our politics springing partly from those lives made us suspicious of it. When disagreements and difficulties occurred and were experienced on the emotional level, I feel that it helped us to remember the fact of our common base being the work we had committed ourselves to do, so that individual feelings were recognised and respected but also referred, when it came to sorting them out, to the work in hand. Nobody cried over the time that we worked together; we managed to put our anger, as well as other things, into words.

The book's arrangement reflects, for me, the looping and darting movement of change that I described above. How can I believe in endings when the five previous stories have poised us on the brink of change, of consciousness moving forwards to grapple with new objects made possible by feminist practice? Here endeth the first reading and the first work, but not, I hope, the second. We are aware of how much work we could still do. Going back over these stories and essays, several questions present themselves: is it important for us to develop new forms? to experiment with existing forms? do we want to relate feminist writing to socialist theories of aesthetics, and if so, how? Do we want an aesthetic into which to fit our work? Other books may develop and attempt to answer these and other questions. Our book demonstrates, rather than this theoretical approach, the practice of feminist writing, and as such will, I hope, provoke many more questions about all the levels of experience of contemporary women. If our writing can not only reflect but also challenge this, our politics will be the stronger for it.

Michele Roberts

Zoë Fairbairns was born in 1948; she studied at St Andrews University and the College of William and Mary in Virginia, USA. Publications include novels, short stories, poetry; also political pamphlets and journalism. From 1975-7 she was information officer at the Women's Research and Resources Centre in London and remains involved in its running; from 1977-8 she was funded by the Greater London Arts Association as Writer-in-Residence at Rutherford School in North London. She has just finished a futuristic novel in which present trends in sexual politics develop into political consequences horrific for women.

Sara Maitland, born in 1950, is a full time writer who has published short stories and some poetry in periodicals and anthologies, both feminist and general. She also works as a journalist. She lives in Swindon, Wiltshire, with her husband and daughter. Her first novel is *Daughter of Jerusalem*, published by Blond and Briggs in September 1978. She is involved in Women's Aid, and is currently working on a book about Women and Christianity.

Valerie Miner is an American writer who has worked in Britain, Canada and the United States. She is co-author of *Her Own Woman* (Macmillan, Canada, 1975) and has published numerous short stories and articles in *Saturday Review, The New Statesman, The Listener, New Society, Spare Rib, Time Out, Maclean's, Saturday Night* and other periodicals. She now teaches at the University of California, Berkeley, in the Field Studies Program. When in London she was active in the National Union of Journalists. She carried that interest back to the States where she now works with Media Alliance, and was one of the founders of the Feminist Writers' Guild.

Michele Roberts read English Language and Literature at Somerville College, Oxford, and then trained as a librarian. Since then she has worked abroad and in London at a variety of jobs. At the moment she earns her living as a computer clerk and is at work on her second novel. She has been involved in the Women's Liberation Movement since 1971. Her first novel is *A Piece of the Night*, published in October 1978 by the Womens Press.

Michelene Wandor has been Poetry Editor and theatre critic for *Time Out* magazine since 1971. She has also written articles and reviews for *Spare Rib*, the feminist monthly magazine. She compiled *The Body Politic*, writings from the Women's Liberation Movement in Britain, 1969-1972, and together with Michele Roberts edited a pamphlet of feminist poetry, *Cutlasses & Earrings*. She also writes plays for the theatre, radio and television; some of her stage plays are published in *Sink Songs*. She has two sons and a degree in English, not necessarily in that order.